Sampler Quilt Blocks

— from —

Native American Designs

Dr. Joyce Mori

SAMPLER QUILT BLOCKS

— from —

NATIVE AMERICAN DESIGNS

Dr. Joyce Mori

American Quilter's Society

P. O. Box 3290 • Paducah, KY 42002-3290

Located in Paducah, Kentucky, the American Quilter's Society (AQS), is dedicated to promoting the accomplishments of today's quilters. Through its publications and events, AQS strives to honor today's quiltmakers and their work – and inspire future creativity and innovation in quiltmaking.

Library of Congress Cataloging-in-Publication Data

Mori, Joyce
    Sampler quilt blocks from Native American designs / Joyce Mori.
        p.   cm.
    ISBN 0-89145-847-6
    1. Patchwork--Patterns. 2. Indian art--Northwest, Pacific-
-Themes, motives.   I. Title.
TT835.M6864   1995
746.46--dc20   95-44170
                                                                   CIP

Additional copies of this book may be ordered from: American Quilter's Society,
P.O. Box 3290, Paducah, KY 42002-3290 @ $14.95. Add $2.00 for postage & handling.

Printed by IMAGE GRAPHICS, INC., Paducah, Kentucky

⇥ ACKNOWLEDGMENTS ⇤

I owe a deep debt of gratitude
to all the Native American craftworkers
who produced the beautiful cornhusk bags
that I used for design ideas.
Their sense of design and use of color are a fantastic source
of inspiration for all quilters.

A special thanks
to the High Desert Museum,
Doris Swayze Bounds Collection, Bend, Oregon,
for letting me see many of the bags in their collection
and for providing photographs for my work.

Many thanks to Victoria Faoro,
Executive Editor of the American Quilter's Society,
and her staff, for doing such an excellent job
with the layout and production
of the three books in this series.
Victoria deserves my deepest appreciation
for publishing these books that provide quilters
with new ideas for designs and quilts.

As always I thank my husband, John,
for his continued support of my work.

I thank God
for my life, abilities, and attitudes
that enable me to pursue work I love.

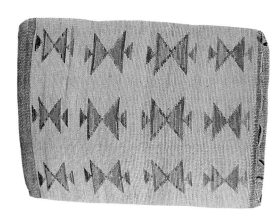

Photo 1.

Photo 2.

❖ CONTENTS ❖

✦ INTRODUCTION ✦

A number of American Indian tribes in the Plateau region (primarily Oregon, Washington, and Idaho) of the United States produced twined storage bags. The Nez Perce, Umatilla, Yakima, Walla Walla, and Wenatchi were some of the tribes making these bags. These tribes were hunters and gatherers, and the bags were used to carry edible tubers, berries, and fish as well as personal possessions.

Originally the bags were made of Indian hemp and bear grass. In more recent times, wool yarns, jute, and string were used in the construction of the bags. Bags were small (6" x 12") to large (20" x 36"). The outsides of the these bags were decorated with vibrant and interesting geometric motifs. Usually the designs woven into the bags were different on each side (see photos 1 and 2, page 5). The technique of false embroidery was used to add the design during weaving. Cornhusks came to be used in the false embroidery, hence the popular name – cornhusk bags.

These bags were highly prized by their owners and were handed down through generations. The earliest bags were decorated with colors of green, yellow, and white. Vegetal dyes provided colors such as purple, blue, green, yellow, orange, red, and black. Commercial aniline dyes expanded the color range used, but red seemed to be a most popular color. A bag often had between two and seven colors. The background color of the bag was medium to light medium beige.

Like other Native American crafts, cornhusk bag making began to die out in the early twentieth century. There are, however, a few weavers making bags today. Unfortunately, this craft has not undergone the strong revival that weaving, pottery, and silvermaking have experienced in the Southwest. Bags take a long time to make; and for this reason, their cost is high. This may be a factor in preventing a major resurgence of the craft.

Although not all the designs utilized on the bags were geometric, naturalistic motifs were very rare. The geometric nature of many of the motifs make them perfect for adaptation to quilt blocks. I studied pictures of many cornhusk bags and created the quilt block designs in this book. The designs often utilized many triangles, and I have provided directions for quick-cutting techniques. There are pages provided in the appendix with the designs presented in black and white line drawings. You can photocopy these and practice coloring them with different color schemes. The blocks pictured in this book include colors that reflect a variety of color ideas – Amish, Christmas, neutrals, spring pastels, Southwest, black and white. There is a tremendous potential for quilters to practice creativity when deciding on the colors to be utilized in the blocks, such as selecting which parts of the blocks to make light or dark. It is also possible to combine blocks for larger overall designs.

Since the blocks in this book contain many triangles, a brief description of several quick-cutting and sewing procedures for triangles is included. However, templates are provided in the appendix section for all the triangles used in the quilt blocks. The first set of instructions deals with half-square triangles. A half-square triangle is one that has a right angle base and two equal sides. In the methods described below, two identical triangles are sewn together to produce a square. This method is not for designs where a triangle is sewn to a square or where the two triangles are not the same size.

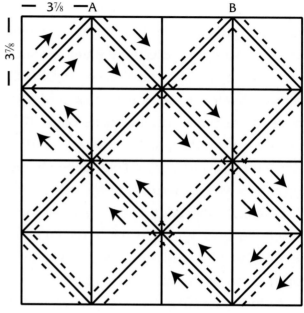

Figure 1.

HALF-SQUARE TRIANGLES

GRID

With this grid method, you draw a grid on your fabric that shows *cutting lines* for the triangles. You must add ⅞" to the size of the finished triangle to determine the dimensions of the grid square. For instance, if you need a 3" (finished size) triangle, the grid must consist of squares that are 3⅞" on the sides. If you are doing a design with 12 half-square triangles of red and green, you would draw a grid with six squares. Remember each square produces two sets of triangles. Depending on the piece of fabric you have, your grid could be two squares on one side and three squares on the other side or one square on one side and six squares on the other.

Draw the grid on the wrong side of the lightest piece of fabric you are using. You can use an ordinary lead pencil for this (see Fig. 1). Next, on every other diagonal row of squares, draw a diagonal line corner to corner through the squares. Figure 1 shows these lines in solid black. On the remaining sets of squares draw a diagonal line from the two opposite corners. Study Figure 1 to determine how to draw the diagonal lines if your grid is not identical to the one in the drawing.

These grid lines, the diagonals and sides, are the cutting lines used when the sewing is complete. The sewing lines are shown in dotted lines on the drawing. These sewing lines are ¼" on both sides of the diagonal lines. You can mark these in pencil if your presser foot or machine needle setting does not give you an accurate ¼" seam.

Place your unmarked piece of fabric right-side up on your worktable and lay your marked piece of fabric, right-side down and marked-side up, over the first piece of fabric. Pin these together in a few places and then sew your diagonal lines. If you start at point A and follow the arrows, you will sew in a continuous line back to A. You are actually sewing on the dotted lines which are ¼" on either side of your marked line. You must sew on both dotted lines. Do the same from point B. Cut the squares and triangles apart on the marked pencil lines when your sewing is complete.

Iron the two triangles open and use a rotary cutter to trim the square to size if necessary. Usually this method is very accurate and trimming is not needed.

STENCIL

Determine the finished size triangle you need and select the appropriate stencil. Several firms make stencils with grids. I use stencils from Needletec ©1988 by Joyce Peaden, and the address is Needletec, 910 Roza Vista Dr., Prosser, WA 99350. Place the wrong side of the fabric up and use a pencil to mark in the slots of the stencil for the number of triangles you will need. Lift the stencil from the fabric and use a pencil and ruler to fill in the diagonal grid. Place the two fabrics together as in the previous method. *Sew carefully on the marked diagonal lines.* I use the open-toe appliqué foot on my machine so I can clearly see the lines. When the sewing is complete, I use a rotary cutter or scissors to cut between the two lines of stitching.

Remember in this method, the stencil gives you the sewing lines for the diagonal markings. Iron and trim as in the grid method.

BIAS STRIP METHOD

With this method bias strips are cut from two fabrics and the strips are sewn together. Squares (consisting of two equal triangles) are then cut from the sewn strips. First you must determine the size of the bias strip you need to cut. If you want a finished square (not including seam allowances) to be 2", you should cut 2¼" strips. The size of the finished square also equals the finished side of the triangle you want.

To cut the first bias angle from the fabric, place the two pieces of fabric for the triangles right sides together on your worktable. Place a right-angle triangle at the top left-hand corner and cut along the long (hypotenuse) line (see Fig. 2). Your plastic triangle ruler will probably not be long enough for the entire cut, so use your plastic ruler to provide the edge for the remainder of the cut. Next cut the bias strips by aligning a clear see-through plastic ruler along the bias edge. Remember, if you want a

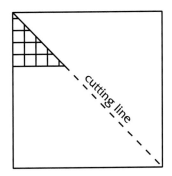

Figure 2.

finished square to be 2", not including the seam allowances, cut the strips 2¼" wide.

Sew down one length of the strips with a ¼" seam. Open the strip. Press the seam allowance toward the darker fabric. The piece of fabric will look like Figure 3. Use a plastic square template and align the diagonal line (45-degree line) directly over the seam line. Trim the right side (see Fig. 4). Next, flip the strip so the trimmed edge is at the left. Take the square plastic template and lay it on the two-fabric strip with the marking for the 2½" line on the left edge of the strip (darker line on Fig. 5). This size represents the size of the bias square including the seam allowances. Make sure that the 45-degree-angle marking on the plastic template lines up on the exact line of the seam. Cut along the two sides.

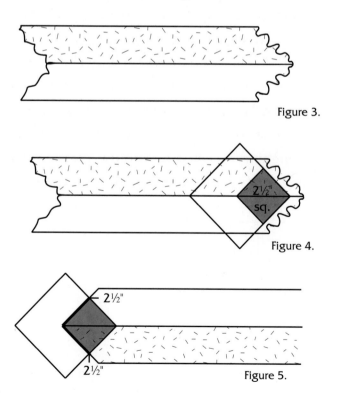

Figure 3.

Figure 4.

Figure 5.

For the next square, move the template across the strip until the 2½" mark is at the end of the seam (see Fig. 6). Cut the edges as before and repeat the process by flipping the fabric to your left. Continue this process until you have cut all the squares you can from the strip of fabric.

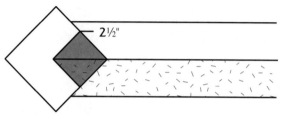

Figure 6.

HALF SQUARES

This method involves cutting strips (but not bias strips) from the fabric and then cutting squares from the strips and triangles from the squares. If you want 2" finished-size triangles, add ⅞" and cut strips that are 2⅞" wide. From this strip, cut a series of squares 2⅞" on a side. Then cut the squares in half along the diagonal. Sew these triangles together along the diagonal. Your finished triangles will be 2" on the side.

This method works very well when you want to make a block from scraps, but do not want to spend time drawing and cutting each triangle. You can cut just two squares from scraps of fabric and cut along the diagonal and sew the triangles together. Your finished product will be two squares each made of half-square triangles.

Easy Angle™ Tool

This is a right-angle hard plastic template marked off in half-inch grids. For a 2" finished-size triangle, cut strips 2½" wide. Square off one end of the strip. Place the triangle template with the 2½" mark at the left side of the strip. Cut along the hypotenuse. The result is a 2" finished-size triangle.

Each method has its positive points. Basically, you have to decide which method is easiest and most accurate for you and which is quicker considering the number of blocks you will be making and the number of triangles you need. If you are just making one block, it is often quickest to use a template since so few triangles are involved. One thing you need to remember for any method is to *handle the triangles as little as possible.* They have bias edges that can stretch and cause accuracy problems.

My No-template Method

I developed a method for quickly cutting the long narrow triangles used in some of the blocks in this book. Directions are provided for a triangle that is 4" (finished size) on one side, by 5" (finished size) on the other. Cut a strip of fabric 5⅝" wide. You are adding ⅝" to the finished size of any one side of the triangle you will need. I usually choose to cut my strip the width of the longest side. Five inches is the longest side of a triangle that is 4" x 5". If the triangle was 2" x 4" finished size, the strip would be cut 4⅝" wide.

Square off one end of this fabric strip and place it wrong-side up on the cutting board. Measure over 4⅝". This is ⅝" wider than the finished size of the other side of the triangle. Put a tiny pencil mark there that is ⅜" up from the bottom edge of the strip (point 1 on Fig. 7). With a clear ruler measure over ⅜" from the outside edge on the top left corner of the fabric strip and make a tiny mark (point 2 on Fig. 7). Cut on the diagonal line between points 1 and 2 (cutting line 3 on Fig. 7). You do not need to mark this line with a pencil. Just place the ruler edge on the two points and cut. This makes one triangle.

Next, measure ⅜" over on the bottom edge of the fabric strip (point 4 on Fig. 7). Be sure you line up one of the horizontal lines of the ruler with the top edge of the fabric. Cut straight up from point 4 (see cutting line 5 on Fig. 7). This makes a second triangle.

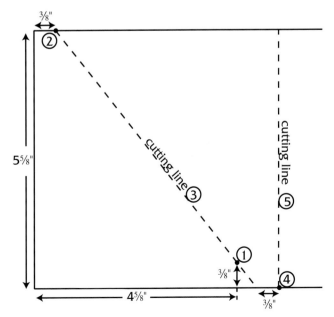

Figure 7.

On designs where the triangles are reversed, there needs to be an adjustment to the above directions in order to achieve both types of triangles. Since the previous triangles were marked and cut with the wrong side of the fabric facing you, simply turn the fabric over, and mark and cut on the right side of the fabric. Follow the exact directions given previously. You will now have both sets of triangles. Do the turning over of the fabric with each color in the set of triangles.

A second technique cuts both angles at the same time. Fold the strip of fabric in half. It does not matter whether you have folded your fabric right sides together or wrong sides together. Trim off the unfolded end. Turn the strip so the cut end is to your left. Follow the directions given. Both sets of triangles are completed at the same time. Once again, do this with the second fabric color in your set.

When you sew the triangles together, use a scant $1/4$" seam. Check the finished measurement. Trim if necessary. With this method, the set of triangles often has to be trimmed on one or two sides a slight amount. I find this very small excess of fabric allows the triangle set to always be trimmed to the exact size needed. This method works quickly on blocks where there are several sizes of triangles. You do not have to trace and utilize a template. However, templates are provided for those quilters who prefer to use them.

ACCURACY

Accuracy is important when cutting and sewing the individual elements of quilt blocks. However, you may not end up with a finished-size triangle that is exactly 4" x 5" no matter which method you use. There are several reasons for this. The thickness of pencil lines made when drawing around templates affects the finished size. The placement of the line on a plastic ruler can determine the dimensions of a finished unit. For example, do you place the black line of the plastic ruler directly on the cut edge of the fabric or do you place the line so it is on the inside or outside of the cut edge? Do you sew an exact $1/4$" seam? You can set your machine at a certain seam setting, but then you must make sure the edge of the presser foot always is directly at the edge of the fabric. You should not be able to see any fabric sticking out.

I think we develop habits using systems that are easiest for us to see and manipulate. And a combination of all these factors can affect the finished size of all the units. I do not see a problem with these variations in size as long as what you do is always the same. For example, if you always place a measuring line on a plastic template just to the right edge of the fabric rather than to the left or down the center, always do it the same way. Always set the needle position at the same setting when sewing on quilt pieces. It may not be a true $1/4$", but even if it is off ever so slightly, it will always be off the same amount. Consistency is the goal.

Plans for twenty 18-inch blocks are included in this section. They can be used in sampler quilts or wallhangings. For each wall quilt there is a color photograph. Also provided is a shaded black and white drawing keyed to the specific colors I used.

Read pages 53 and 54 for more information on construction of the blocks. In general, it is to be noted that triangles are sewn together to form squares or rectangles. Then additional squares or rectangles are sewn onto these units. The designs are usually built up by rows and the rows are sewn together to complete a block. Highly detailed sewing instructions are not needed with these drawings. In fact, there is often more than one way to join the units within the block to complete the entire design. Add the borders for the project once the block has been sewn.

Each block and border design for the projects is also shown as a black and white drawing in the section immediately following the projects. Photocopy these pages and experiment with placing color, combining blocks, and interchanging border selections. All of the blocks are unique in design. There are endless possibilities for combining blocks, for repeating blocks in an all-over design, and for using blocks as single units. Borders can be interchanged between the different blocks because the blocks are all identical in size – 18" x 18". It is simply a matter of which borders work best with which blocks.

IMPORTANT CUTTING DIRECTIONS

All pieces are described by finished size. Exact-size templates for the triangles are provided in the appendix. I encourage quick-cutting methods when possible. Just remember to add appropriate seam allowances. This applies to squares and rectangles also. If the directions call for a 3" x 8" rectangle and if you wish to rotary cut it, you would cut the piece 3½" x 8½". Likewise, if you draw the template, remember to add ¼" seam allowance to *all* sides.

The amounts of fabric required in each color for a single project are under ¼ yard in most cases. Often only scraps are needed for some colors. Therefore, only cases where the fabric amounts are over ¼ yard are noted. Fabric amounts specified are generous.

Block and border piece requirements are separated to make it easy for you to switch blocks from one border to another.

When the requirements call for eight each Template T, Tr, this means cut eight from the template (Template T) and then cut eight more by flipping the template over (Template Tr).

Be sure to read all directions before starting a project. Also check the finished measurements of the block. As I mentioned in the previous section there can be slight variations in the finished size of a block. If your block is not 18½" x 18½", you will have to make adjustments in the size requirements given for the border pieces.

Remember to add ¼" seam allowance to all templates, even the square and rectangle sizes. The sizes given for the triangles, rectangles, and squares are finished sizes. When the directions read 4 Template T and Tr, it means cut 4 from Template T and then cut four more by flipping the Template over (Template Tr).

PROJECT #1 – 22" x 22"

CUTTING INSTRUCTIONS

Block:

Template T, Tr – 4 each madras stripe, 4 each background

Template K, Kr – 4 each background, 4 each light plaid

3" x 3" square – 4 background

2" x 12" rectangle – 2 madras stripe

Template J, Jr – 2 each stripe, 2 each background

3" x 8" rectangle – 2 background

2" x 8" rectangle – 1 background

2" x 3" rectangle – 2 background

Border:

Template H – 32 background, 12 dark gray stripe, 14 stripe, 18 light plaid

FABRIC REQUIREMENTS

Except for the madras stripe, these fabrics were cutaways from shirt factories. If you are doing only the block, ¼ yard is enough for the background; but it takes almost ½ yard of the background fabric if you include the border design.

SEWING DIRECTIONS

Sew the block first. Begin by sewing the triangles together to form squares or rectangles. Sew the squares and rectangles to the T, Tr triangle units (Row 1). Sew the K and Kr triangle units, placing the small rectangle between them to make Unit 1. Sew the Jr and J triangle units together. Sew the rectangle between each set of J, Jr's (Unit 2). Sew a long rectangle to each side of Unit 2.

Sew a Unit 1 to each side of that unit. Sew Row 1 to the top and bottom of this section. Your block is complete. The border is added after the block is finished.

QUILTING

This piece was machine quilted. The background of the block is free motion stipple quilting. The parallel lines on the large stripe triangles are ½" apart. On the corners of the border, the quilting lines are ½" from the outer edge. Only the patterned fabrics of the border are quilted down the middle of the diamond-shaped design. The plain background sections are left plain and are not even quilted in the ditch. If you enjoy machine quilting, more quilting lines can be added.

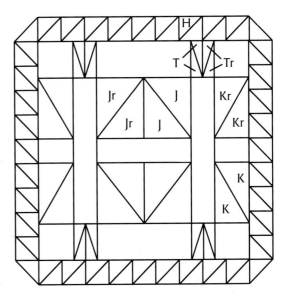

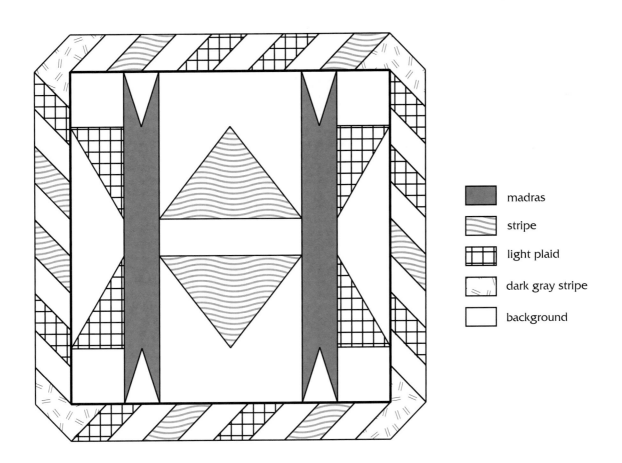

madras

stripe

light plaid

dark gray stripe

background

✦ PROJECT #2 ✦

Remember to add ¼" seam allowance to all templates, even the square and rectangle sizes. The sizes given for the triangles, rectangles, and squares are finished sizes. When the directions read 4 Template T and Tr, it means cut 4 from Template T and then cut four more by flipping the Template over (Template Tr).

Project #2 – 24" x 24"

CUTTING INSTRUCTIONS

Block:

Template P, Pr – 4 each dark blue, 4 each background
Template H – 16 each dark blue, 16 each background
2" x 2" square – 12 dark blue, 2 background
2" x 3" rectangle – 4 background
3" x 6" rectangle – 2 background
2" x 1" rectangle – 8 background
2" x 4" rectangle – 4 background

Border:

Template A – 8 dark blue, 8 background
Template P, Pr – 10 each dark blue, 10 each background
2" x 3" rectangle – 4 background

3" x 6" rectangle – 2 background

FABRIC REQUIREMENTS

The dark blue fabrics are assorted small scrap pieces. One-half yard of the background fabric is needed for the block and its border.

SEWING DIRECTIONS

Begin by sewing the triangles together to form squares or rectangles. To simplify the sewing directions a square made from two A triangles will be called square A; a rectangle formed from two Pr triangles will be called rectangle Pr. The line drawing shows that the quilt can be broken down into 10 horizontal rows. Working from left to right, sew square A to a rectangle. Sew a Pr rectangle to this. Add a P rectangle. Add a large rectangle. Sew on a Pr rectangle, a P rectangle, a small rectangle, and a square A. Row 1 is complete. Complete rows 2 through 10 in the same way. The block and the border are thus sewn at the same time.

QUILTING

The background of this wall quilt was quilted in parallel lines spaced 1" apart. The blue pieces of the block have outline quilting set in ½" from the outside of the pieces. The blue pieces of the border have parallel lines, spaced ½" apart, going from top to bottom of each triangle. The corners were left unquilted.

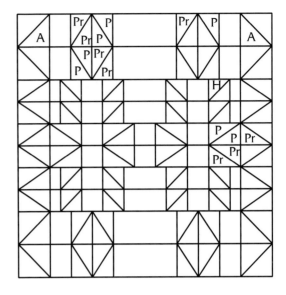

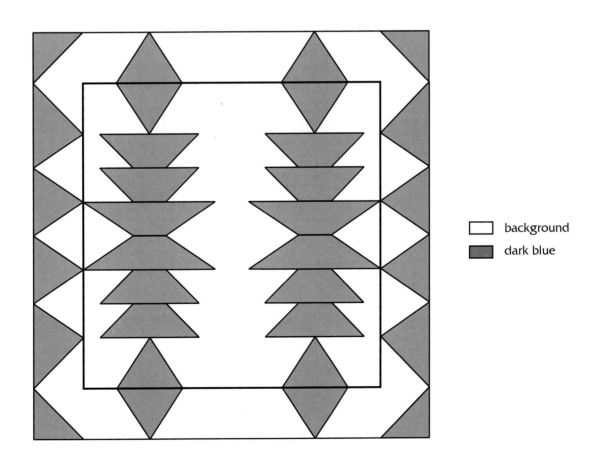

background
dark blue

✦ PROJECT #3 ✦

> Remember to add ¼" seam allowance to all templates, even the square and rectangle sizes. The sizes given for the triangles, rectangles, and squares are finished sizes.
>
> When the directions read 4 Template T and Tr, it means cut 4 from Template T and then cut four more by flipping the Template over (Template Tr).

Project #3 – 28" x 28"

CUTTING INSTRUCTIONS

Block:

    3" x 6" rectangle – 4 orange print

    Template A – 12 teal, 16 border stripe, 16 gold, 4 teal print

    3" x 3" square – 4 orange print

Border:

    1" x 18" rectangle – 4 pale orange, 2 stripe

    1" x 20" rectangle – 2 pale orange

    1" x 24" rectangle – 2 stripe

    1" x 28" rectangle – 2 pale orange

    1" x 1" square – 4 teal

    1" x 4" rectangle – 28 pale orange, 4 teal

    1" x 3" rectangle – 20 teal

    1" x 2" rectangle – 4 teal, 4 stripe

FABRIC REQUIREMENTS

    In this block, the patterned squares were cut from a border stripe. I used a plastic template for accurate placement of the stripes (see Fig. 8). Four units of A triangles are combined to make a square. Depending on the specific stripe fabric, you may be able to use four B triangles to make another square that is similar, though not identical, to the square made from triangle A.

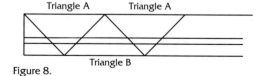

Figure 8.

These triangles use template A. The width of the stripe, the repeat, and placement of the triangle template all affect the amount of fabric required. However, a half yard of fabric should be sufficient.

SEWING DIRECTIONS

Sew the block first. Follow the diagram and sew the A's together to form squares. Add rectangles or squares where necessary to form rows. Sew these six rows together to form the block.

The border for this block is made up of 5 separate rows. Sew the side borders first. Sew each row individually, and then join them into a five-row unit. Sew one of these units onto each side of the wall quilt.

Complete the first two inner rows of the top and bottom borders. Once they are sewn together, sew the small rectangle to each end of these two-row units. Sew row three onto this two-row unit and add the end rectangles. Continue until you have completed all five rows of the top and bottom borders. Sew a five-row unit onto the top and bottom of the quilt.

QUILTING

Motif 4 was quilted in the gold squares and in the teal print square of the block. It is reduced and modified from a design in *Quilting Patterns from Native American Designs* published by the American Quilter's Society. Put a row or two of quilting in the squares made from the constructed stripe fabric. Follow the lines on the fabric. The border is quilted in the ditch and the teal pieces have lines of quilting that are set in $\frac{1}{4}$" from the outside edges.

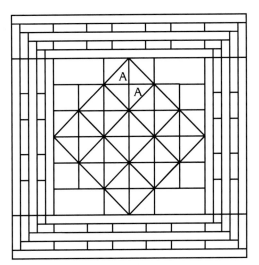

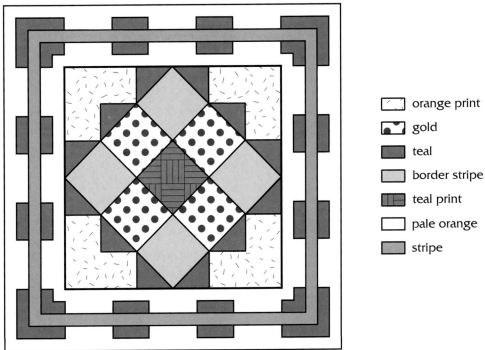

orange print	
gold	
teal	
border stripe	
teal print	
pale orange	
stripe	

→ PROJECT #4 ←

Remember to add ¼"
seam allowance to all
templates, even the
square and rectangle
sizes. The sizes given
for the triangles, rec-
tangles, and squares
are finished sizes.
When the directions
read 4 Template T
and Tr, it means cut 4
from Template T and
then cut four more by
flipping the Template
over (Template Tr).

Project #4 – 30" x 30"

CUTTING INSTRUCTIONS

Block:

2" x 6" rectangle – 4 background print, 2 dark green
print

2" x 4" rectangle – 4 background print

2" x 2" square – 4 background print, 4 medium green
print

Template H – 12 background print, 4 dark green
print, 8 medium green print

Template A – 4 background print, 4 medium green
print, 8 dark purple print

Template I – 4 dark green print

1" x 3" rectangle – 4 dark purple print

1" x 4" rectangle – 2 purple solid, 2 peach solid, 2
lilac solid

Border:

1" x 1" square – 4 dark purple print

1" x 18" rectangle – 4 off white

2" x 2" square – 4 lilac

2" x 20" rectangle – 4 medium green print

3" x 3" square – 4 dark green print

3" x 24" rectangle – 4 background

FABRIC REQUIREMENTS

The background print for this project is a large mul-
ticolored pastel print. It gives a soft spring touch to the
design. You will need a fat quarter of the background
fabric and scraps of the other colors. If you choose to
add this border, you will need to increase the background fabric to ½ yard.

SEWING DIRECTIONS

Sew the block together first. If you study the diagram carefully, you will see that this block consists of four horizontal rows. Sew two H's together to form a square. Sew a rectangle to this (unit 1). Sew an H to each side of a square. Sew this to I. Sew two H's together. Sew a square to this. Sew a rectangle to the top of this H/H unit and square. This is now sewn to the H/I unit. Sew unit 1 onto this. Repeat this entire process. A rectangle is sewn between two of these units to form row 1.

Now sew A's together to form squares and then sew a rectangle between these squares. Repeat. Sew three rectangles together and attach these between the A squares unit. This is row 2. Complete the block by finishing rows three and four.

The border consists of three separate rows. Sew the side of each row first and then add the top and bottom. Repeat for each row of the border.

QUILTING

The parallel background lines in the block are spaced ½" apart. The other lines on the block are spaced 1" from the outside and inside edges of the border.

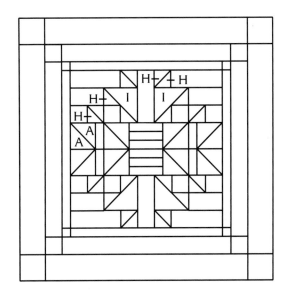

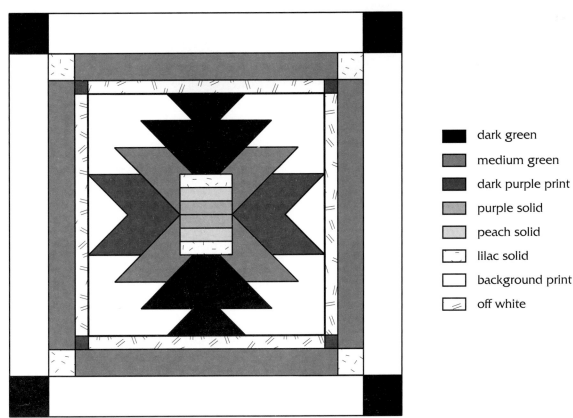

■	dark green
▨	medium green
▨	dark purple print
▨	purple solid
▨	peach solid
▨	lilac solid
□	background print
▨	off white

✦ PROJECT #5 ✦

Project #5 – 27" x 27"

CUTTING INSTRUCTIONS

Block:
- 2" x 6" rectangle – 4 black
- 3" x 4" rectangle – 4 black
- Template P, Pr – 2 each black, 2 each peach
- Template K, Kr – 2 each black, 2 each turquoise
- Template F, Fr – 2 each black, 2 each purple

Border:
- 1" x 18" rectangle – 2 black
- 1" x 20" rectangle – 2 black
- 2" x 2" square – 4 black
- 2" x 20" rectangle – 4 constructed fabric
- 1½" x 1½" square – 2 peach, 2 purple
- 1½" x 24" rectangle – 4 black

Remember to add ¼" seam allowance to all templates, even the square and rectangle sizes. The sizes given for the triangles, rectangles, and squares are finished sizes. When the directions read 4 Template T and Tr, it means cut 4 from Template T and then cut four more by flipping the Template over (Template Tr).

FABRIC REQUIREMENTS

Allow ⅓ yard of black for the block only, but ½ yard if you are adding the border. I call the multicolor fabric in the border constructed fabric. Gather Amish-colored scraps and strips from this and other projects and sew them randomly together. When you have a long enough piece, trim it to the correct size and use the scraps from this to start on another strip. Do not worry about bias edges.

SEWING DIRECTIONS

Sew the block first. This block consists of six horizontal rows. Sew Pr to Pr to form a rectangle. Sew a rectangle to this. Sew P to P and sew a rectangle to this. Sew the Pr/P units together to form the first row. Repeat this basic process for the other rows to complete the block.

Sew a black rectangle to the top and bottom of the block. Then add black rectangles to the two sides. Cut your strips of constructed fabric to the proper size. Sew a black square onto the ends of two of these constructed fabric pieces. Sew a constructed fabric piece to the top and bottom of the wall quilt. Then sew the constructed fabric rows with the squares attached to each side of the quilt. Complete the final border in the same manner.

QUILTING

The constructed fabric is difficult to hand quilt because there are so many seams. This is a perfect area to freehand machine quilt. This project is quilted in the ditch by machine around all the border sections made of constructed fabric. The triangles in the block are outline quilted with a spacing of ½". Quilting motif number 5 is used in the block. The inside black border has a quilting line down the middle. The outside black border has quilting lines set in ¼" from the outside and inside edges.

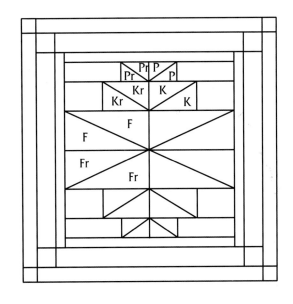

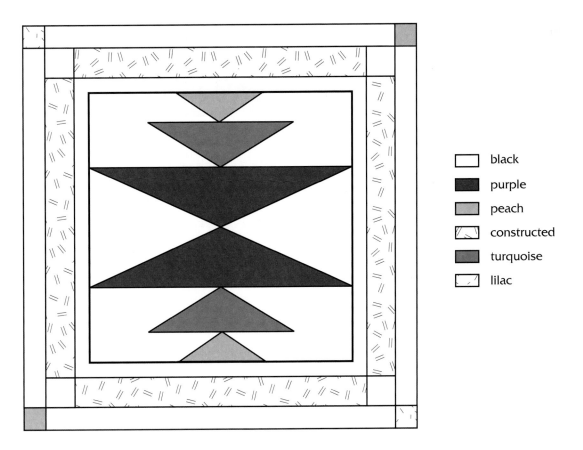

black

purple

peach

constructed

turquoise

lilac

Remember to add ¼" seam allowance to all templates, even the square and rectangle sizes. The sizes given for the triangles, rectangles, and squares are finished sizes. When the directions read 4 Template T and Tr, it means cut 4 from Template T and then cut four more by flipping the Template over (Template Tr).

Project #6 – 28" x 28"

CUTTING INSTRUCTIONS

Block:

    2" x 3" rectangle – 1 black, 1 white

    2" x 2" square – 12 black, 10 white

    2" x 5" rectangle – 3 black, 3 white

    2" x 6" rectangle – 4 black, 1 white

    2" x 7" rectangle – 3 black, 3 white

    2" x 1" rectangle – 2 black

    2" x 4" rectangle – 2 white

Border:

    1" x 1" square – 4 b/w print

    1" x 18" rectangle – 4 light gray

    2" x 8" rectangle – 8 dark gray print, 8 black print

Template H – 16 b/w stripe, 8 dark gray print

2" x 2" square – 4 b/w print, 8 b/w stripe

2" x 4" rectangle – 4 b/w stripe

If you use a black and white stripe as indicated on this project, use a plastic template to cut the squares, triangles, and rectangles. This allows you to match the stripes to get a miter at the corner and to achieve a match between the outer and middle border rows. Study the photograph to see the direction of the lines of the stripe.

FABRIC REQUIREMENTS

    The block requires a fat quarter of black and a fat

quarter of white. The fabric amounts for the border are under a quarter yard. However, it is advisable to have a quarter yard of the black and white stripe just in case you make some mistakes in cutting out the triangles or in trying to match the stripes.

SEWING DIRECTIONS

The block consists of nine horizontal rows. Each row is constructed of only squares and rectangles. Follow the diagram carefully to note the placement of each color of square or rectangle.

The border consists of three separate rows. Add each row separately. Sew each side, then the top and bottom.

QUILTING

This piece is machine quilted. Quilting in the ditch is done between each of the border rows. A single line of stitching was done down the middle of the black

print row and the dark gray print row. In the block, quilting is done down the middle of the white pieces. The black pieces have two rows of quilting with each row set in ½" from the outside and inside edges.

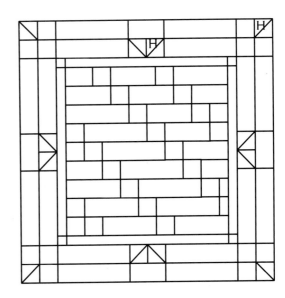

- ☐ white
- ☐ stripe
- ☐ light gray
- ☐ black and white print
- ▨ dark gray print
- ■ black print and black solid

Remember to add ¼"
seam allowance to all
templates, even the
square and rectangle
sizes. The sizes given
for the triangles, rec-
tangles, and squares
are finished sizes.
When the directions
read 4 Template T
and Tr, it means cut 4
from Template T and
then cut four more by
flipping the Template
over (Template Tr).

Project #7 – 26" x 26"

CUTTING INSTRUCTIONS
Block:
  4" x 5" rectangle – 4 beige
  Template I – 4 dark print, 4 beige
  1" x 10" rectangle – 2 beige
  Template J, Jr – 4 each stripe, 2 each beige, 2 each
    dark print

Border:
  2" x 2" square – 4 black print, 4 beige
  1" x 1" square – 8 black print, 4 beige
  1" x 4" rectangle – 4 black print, 4 beige
  1" x 2" rectangle – 16 black print
  1" x 3" rectangle – 8 black print, 8 beige
  1" x 10" rectangle – 8 beige

  1" x 7" rectangle – 8 beige
  1" x 8" rectangle – 4 beige
  1" x 12" rectangle – 4 beige

This block was made from two closely related
Native American patterned fabrics. One is a modified
stripe, and the other is a print. The design of this block
resembles motifs found on Native American pottery
and rugs as well as cornhusk bags.

FABRIC REQUIREMENTS
Two different black fabrics are used in the border,
but that is not necessary. If you use only one black
print, you would need less than ¼ yard. The beige used
in the border is a different beige than that utilized in

the block. One-half yard of a beige is needed for the block and border combined.

SEWING DIRECTIONS

The block consists of three horizontal rows. The middle row contains the J and Jr units with a rectangle on either end.

The border for this quilt consists of four rows. The first two rows are sewn together before being sewn to the block. Attach the side borders first. Then add the top and bottom. Sew the last two rows together before sewing them to the wall quilt. Sew the sides on first and then the top and bottom.

QUILTING

Crosshatch quilting is done on the background area of the block. The lines are spaced 1" apart.

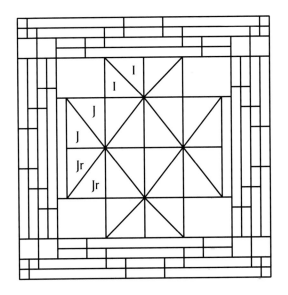

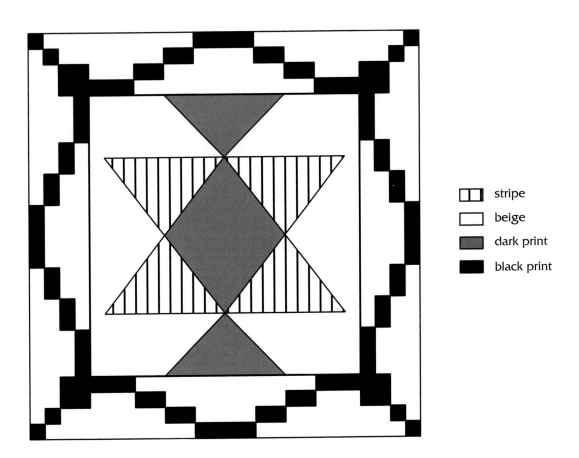

	stripe
	beige
	dark print
	black print

→ PROJECT #8 ←

Project #8 – 30" x 30"

CUTTING INSTRUCTIONS

Block:

    5" x 5" square – 4 background

    2" x 2" square – 1 lilac

    Template J – 4 green print, 4 background

    Template Jr – 4 marbled, 4 background

    Template I – 4 marbled, 4 green print

Border:

    Template B – 8 marbled, 8 green solid

    2" x 2" square – 12 rose, 8 green solid

    2" x 4" rectangle – 8 green solid

    1" x 5" rectangle – 8 green solid

    Template H – 32 green solid, 32 background

    4" x 4" square – 4 background

The template H triangles can be constructed easily with the half-square triangle technique.

FABRIC REQUIREMENTS

One-half yard of the background fabric is needed to complete both the block and border. One-half yard of the green solid is required for the border. The other amounts are under ¼ yard.

SEWING DIRECTIONS

Sew the block first. The block contains four rows. Sew Jr's together to form a rectangle. Sew J's together to form a rectangle. Add a square to each of these. Sew these units together to complete a row. Complete the other three rows of the block. The lilac square in the center of the block is appliquéd in place after the block has been sewn together.

The center pieced unit of each border section is sewn first. Study the diagram to see how the other units are attached.

QUILTING

Background meander quilting is done on the green solid of the border. The lines on the rose squares are ¼" apart. On the marbled triangles of the border the lines are spaced ¾" apart.

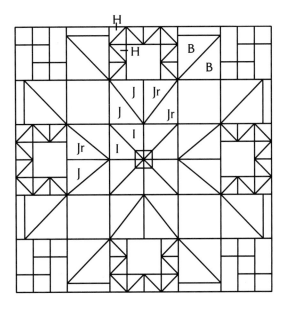

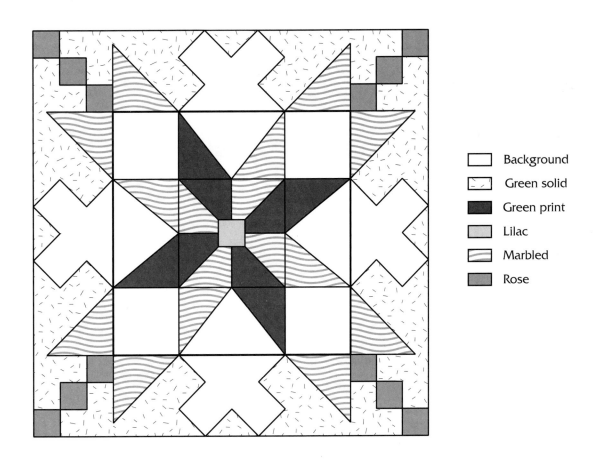

☐	Background
☐	Green solid
■	Green print
☐	Lilac
☰	Marbled
☐	Rose

✦ PROJECT #9 ✦

Project #9 – 26" x 26"

Remember to add ¼" seam allowance to all templates, even the square and rectangle sizes. The sizes given for the triangles, rectangles, and squares are finished sizes.

When the directions read 4 Template T and Tr, it means cut 4 from Template T and then cut four more by flipping the Template over (Template Tr).

CUTTING INSTRUCTIONS

Block:

Template A – 24 from rust, gold, and orange scraps; 12 from green scraps, 12 light beige

1" x 18" rectangle – 2 light beige

1" x 3" rectangle – 12 from rust, gold, and orange scraps

2" x 3" rectangle – 6 from green scraps

Border:

1" x 18" rectangle – 8 medium beige

4" x 4" square – 4 medium beige

Template P/Pr – 12 each medium beige, 12 each dark green

Appliqué tree and stem – 4 each

FABRIC REQUIREMENTS

These are all small amounts of fabrics. You could even use scraps of beige instead of only one beige fabric. A fat quarter of beige is more than enough if you choose a single beige color. For the border a fat quarter of the dark green and medium beige is sufficient.

SEWING INSTRUCTIONS

The block consists of six horizontal rows. Once you have completed the rows and have sewn them together, add a beige strip to each side of the block.

The border consists of rectangles formed by sewing two P's together and two Pr's together. Beige strips are sewn to the top and bottom of the strip constructed of P/Pr rectangular units. The tree designs in

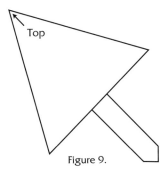

Figure 9.

each corner of the border are appliquéd onto the beige background. The pattern is included on page 65.

HANGING LOOPS

These loops are constructed of a plastic material that resembles leather. Each is $1\frac{1}{2}$" x $6\frac{1}{2}$". They are sewn in place before the project is quilted. Lay the batting on a flat surface and place the completed project on top of it, right-side up. Pin the loops in place on top of these layers. The loops are placed on top of the quilt top. Space them evenly. Place the backing on top of this bundle, right-side down. Pin this bundle (batting, quilt top, loops, and backing) across the top edge. Sew this with a $\frac{1}{4}$" seam. Then flip the backing to the back. The loops will be up in their hanging position. Baste the

quilt sandwich together as you normally would prior to quilting. When the quilting is complete, binding is sewn only to the two sides and bottom of the quilt.

QUILTING

The appliquéd trees in the corners of the border are quilted in the ditch around their outside edges. The parallel lines on the dark green border are spaced $\frac{3}{4}$" apart as are the lines on the medium beige of the border triangles. The lines on the orange, gold, and rust scraps of the block were spaced $\frac{1}{2}$" apart.

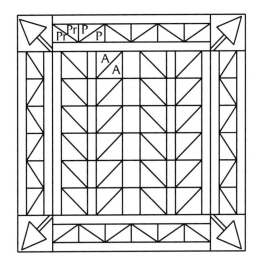

	shades of green
	shades of orange, gold, brown
	light beige
	beige

Project #10 – 26" x 26"

Remember to add ¼" seam allowance to all templates, even the square and rectangle sizes. The sizes given for the triangles, rectangles, and squares are finished sizes.
When the directions read 4 Template T and Tr, it means cut 4 from Template T and then cut four more by flipping the Template over (Template Tr).

CUTTING INSTRUCTIONS

Block:

    1" x 2" rectangle – 6 navy, 4 light spatter
    2" x 2" square – 12 navy, 13 light spatter, 2 multi-pattern, 6 background
    2" x 6" rectangle – 2 multi-pattern, 4 background
    1" x 8" rectangle – 4 background
    2" x 4" rectangle – 6 background
    1" x 10" rectangle – 2 multi-pattern

Border:

    Template I – 4 background
    2" x 2" square – 32 background
    2" x 4" rectangle – 4 background
    Template H – 36 background, 44 navy

FABRIC REQUIREMENTS

The block is made entirely from hand-dyed fabrics. Only small amounts of fabric are required. The background fabric for the border is a rust solid and is slightly lighter than the mottled rust used as the background of the block. For the border you will need a fat quarter of navy and a half yard of background fabric.

SEWING DIRECTIONS

Sew the block first. The block consists of eleven vertical rows. Study the piecing diagram and complete each row. The border consists of two rows.

QUILTING

Meander quilting is done on the border background. The quilting lines on the navy triangles of the border are spaced ¼" from the edge.

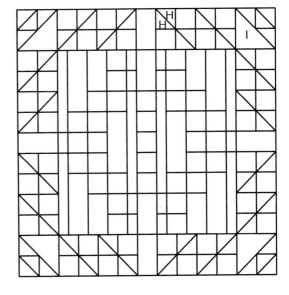

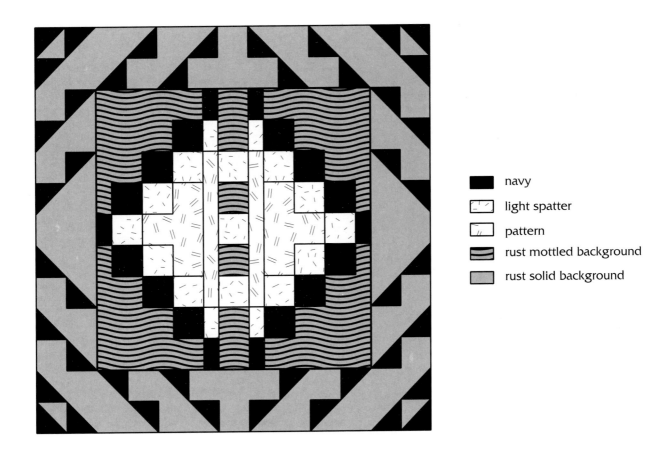

navy
light spatter
pattern
rust mottled background
rust solid background

Project #11 – 26" x 26"

Remember to add ¼" seam allowance to all templates, even the square and rectangle sizes. The sizes given for the triangles, rectangles, and squares are finished sizes. When the directions read 4 Template T and Tr, it means cut 4 from Template T and then cut four more by flipping the Template over (Template Tr).

CUTTING INSTRUCTIONS
Block:
   Template G – 2 rust, 2 floral print
   Template I – 2 rust, 2 floral print
   Template Q, Qr – 3 each rust, 3 each maroon print
   Template 0 – 4 rust, 4 maroon print
   2" x 8" rectangle – 1 floral print, 2 rust
   4" x 6" rectangle – 2 rust
   2" x 6" rectangle – 1 rust
   2" x 3" rectangle – 2 rust
   1" x 7" rectangle – 4 rust

Border:
   1" x 18" rectangle – 4 rust
   1" x 3" rectangle – 8 rust

1" x 8" rectangle – 8 rust
1" x 6" rectangle – 8 rust, 4 floral print
1" x 4" rectangle – 8 rust
1" x 2" rectangle – 4 floral print
3" x 3" square – 4 floral print
1" x 1" square – 4 floral print
1" x 10" rectangle – 4 floral print

FABRIC REQUIREMENTS
   If you wish to make the block and border as shown in this project, you will need ½ yard of the floral print and 1 yard of the rust. The other colors need only small pieces.

SEWING DIRECTIONS
   Sew the block first. Check the piecing diagram

when sewing the quilt together. Sew the G's together to form squares. Sew these two squares together. Sew the I's together to form squares. Sew a rectangle to the top of the two I units. Sew a rectangle to the sides of this I unit. Sew the G squares to this unit. Sew the O's together to form squares. Sew these two squares together and add a rectangle to each side of the squares. Add one of these long units to each side of the G/I unit. Sew the strips consisting of the Q and Qr units and add these to the top and bottom of the block.

The border has four rows. Sew each border together as a four-row unit. Attach the side borders first. Sew the top and bottom borders (these have the corner squares attached to each end) onto the block last.

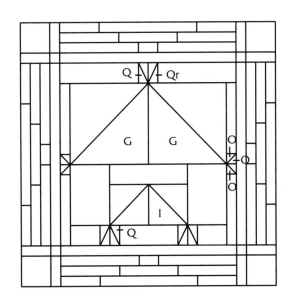

QUILTING

Much of the quilting is in the ditch following the seam lines of all the strips of the border pieces. Motifs #1, #2, and #3 are quilted in the large rust areas of the block. These motifs are found beginning on page 74.

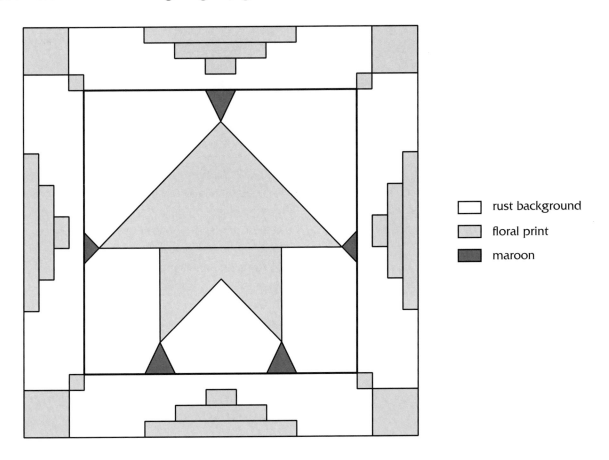

☐ rust background

☐ floral print

■ maroon

Project #12 – 26" x 26"

Remember to add ¼" seam allowance to all templates, even the square and rectangle sizes. The sizes given for the triangles, rectangles, and squares are finished sizes.

When the directions read 4 Template T and Tr, it means cut 4 from Template T and then cut four more by flipping the Template over (Template Tr).

CUTTING INSTRUCTIONS

Block:
  1½" x 18" rectangle – 2 beige, 2 constructed fabric
  1½" x 3" rectangle – 12 dark blue floral, 4 beige, 4 blue floral print
  1½" x 6" rectangle – 4 beige
  Template M, Mr – 10 each rust, 4 each blue floral print, 6 each beige

Border:
  Template I – 20 dark blue, 20 medium beige
  2" x 2" square – 4 medium beige
  Template Q, Qr – 4 each medium beige, 4 each dark blue

FABRIC REQUIREMENTS

Notice that the medium beige in the border is not the same as the beige in the blocks. The same is true for the blue prints. The values are almost equal, and this allows you to use scraps to complete the border. Notice that rows two and nine of the block are made of constructed fabric. I cut 2" strips of the fabric and sewed them randomly together, using a bias seam. I cut the finished strip to the required length. With this technique the strip looks deliberately pieced, but it is not.

SEWING DIRECTIONS

Sew the block first. The block consists of twelve horizontal rows. Two M's or Mr's are sewn together to form a rectangle. Other rectangles are added to form a row. Study the piecing diagram.

For the border, first sew the center section consisting of the Q, Qr triangles and the square. Attach the squares made from the Template I triangle to either side. Follow the piecing diagram.

QUILTING

Parallel line quilting is used all over the quilt. Study the photograph for ideas.

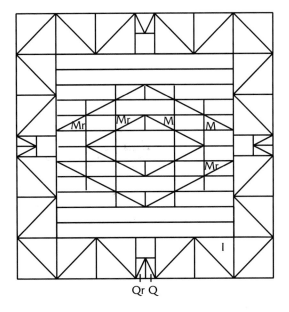

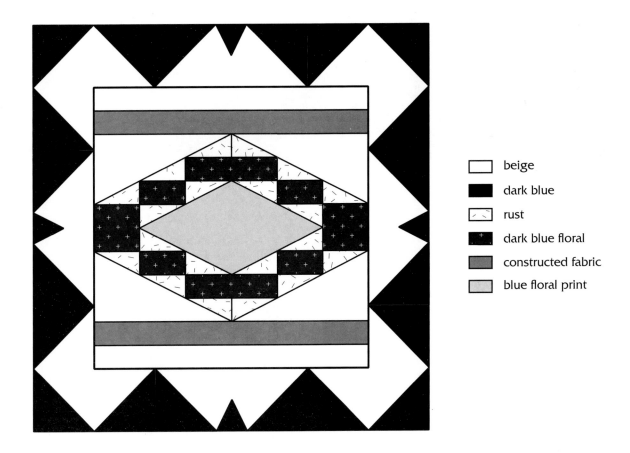

beige

dark blue

rust

dark blue floral

constructed fabric

blue floral print

Project #13 – 50" x 50"

CUTTING INSTRUCTIONS

Block 1 (top left):

Template U – 4 beige, 4 tan

2" x 8" rectangle – 2 tan, 2 black print

Template H – 12 tan, 16 black print, 28 medium orange

2" x 2" square – 1 rust

Block 2 (top right):

3" x 3" square – 2 beige background

3" x 5" rectangle – 7 beige background, 1 medium background print

3" x 3½" rectangle – 2 beige background

3" x 2" rectangle – 5 beige background, 1 medium background print

Remember to add ¼" seam allowance to all templates, even the square and rectangle sizes. The sizes given for the triangles, rectangles, and squares are finished sizes. When the directions read 4 Template T and Tr, it means cut 4 from Template T and then cut four more by flipping the Template over (Template Tr).

3" x 8" rectangle – 1 beige background, 1 medium background print

1½" x 3" rectangle – 4 black

Template M, Mr – 7 each brown print, 7 each yellow

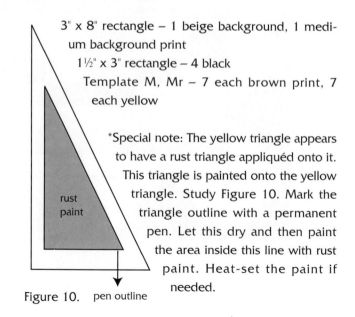

Figure 10.   pen outline

*Special note: The yellow triangle appears to have a rust triangle appliquéd onto it. This triangle is painted onto the yellow triangle. Study Figure 10. Mark the triangle outline with a permanent pen. Let this dry and then paint the area inside this line with rust paint. Heat-set the paint if needed.

Block 3 (Bottom left):

Template Pr – 20 black, 20 rust

3" x 4" rectangle – 14 beige

3" x 2" rectangle – 6 beige

Block 4 (bottom right):

1" x 5" rectangle – 4 black print

2" x 3" rectangle – 4 black print, 4 beige

1" x 2" rectangle – 4 black print, 2 brown floral print

1" x 4" rectangle – 2 black print, 2 brown print

1" x 1" square – 4 brown floral print, 4 beige

2" x 2" square – 8 rust print, 8 brown floral print

1" x 3" rectangle – 4 beige

2" x 4" rectangle – 14 beige

2" x 8" rectangle – 2 beige

Border and sashing:

Drawings for the border of Project #13 do not appear at the back of the book. Any of the blocks in this book would work well with this border arrangement. If you wish to try different colors, use the drawing included with the project directions.

2" x 18" rectangle – 8 brown print, 12 pale gold

2" x 2" square – 12 brown print, 9 rust

2" x 22" rectangle – 8 brown print

2" x 6" rectangle – 4 brown print

FABRIC REQUIREMENTS

For Block 2 the background requires ⅓ yard of fabric. All other colors in the blocks require no more than fat quarters of fabric; and in most cases, scraps of fabric are all that is required.

For the border and sashing the pale gold requires ⅔ yard. One yard is needed of the brown print. The rust is under ¼ yard. If you make your binding from one of the sashing colors, you must allow additional fabric.

SEWING DIRECTIONS

Sew the blocks first. Carefully study the piecing drawings when putting your blocks together. Block 1 is divided into four squares with sashing strips between the squares. Sew seven medium orange Template H units together to form a strip. Sew another strip using the black and tan Template H units. Sew these strips together. Sew a Template U to each side of this. This represents one square. Finish the other three squares and add the strips between them.

Block 2 consists of 6 rows. Sew the Template M triangles together to form rectangles. Repeat with the Template Mr. Attach the required rectangles to complete a row. Sew the rows together to finish the block.

Block 3 is constructed of 6 rows and is sewn together in the same manner as Block 2.

Block 4 has 10 rows. Sew the squares and rectangles together to form each row and then sew the rows together.

Sew the sashing on the sides of the blocks first, then piece the remaining rows of borders and sew them in place. Study the piecing diagram.

QUILTING

Block 1 has special motifs #6 and #7 quilted in the beige and tan areas. The motifs can be found on pages 77 and 78. On Block 2 a line of quilting in black thread is placed on top of the black pen line. Block 3 has motif #8 placed in four of the corner background pieces. Motif #9 is quilted on the edges of the center square. In Block 4, motif #10 is quilted on the background rectangles at the top and bottom of this block. Much of the quilting on these blocks is with parallel lines. Motif #11 is quilted in the brown sashing of this quilt.

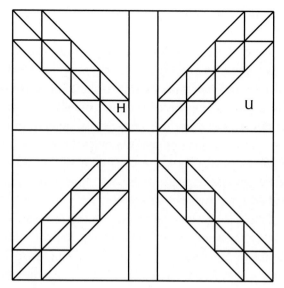

Block 1.

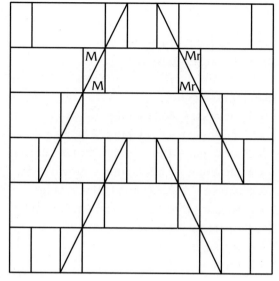

Block 2.

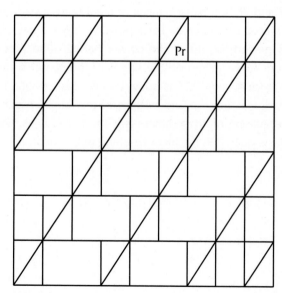

Block 3.

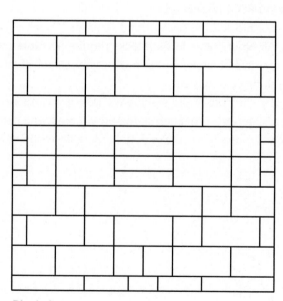

Block 4.

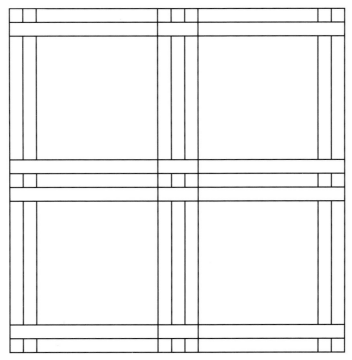

Project 13 border.

pale gold

rust

brown

beige

dark print/black

tan or yellow

medium orange or medium print

brown floral

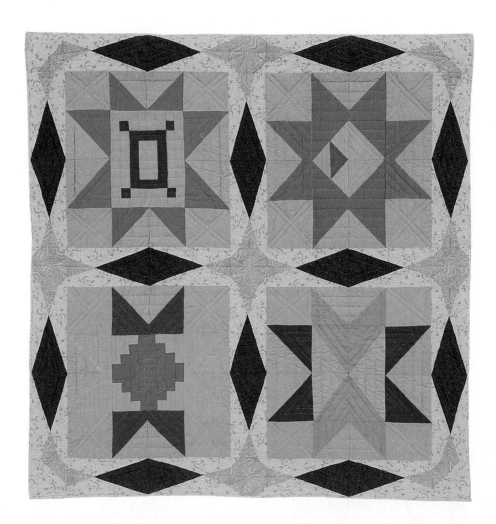

Project #14 – 48" x 48"

CUTTING INSTRUCTIONS

Block 1 (top left):
   Template I – 4 green, 4 tan
   Template B – 4 green, 4 tan
   4" x 5" rectangle – 4 tan
   1" x 10" rectangle – 2 yellow
   1" x 1" square – 4 yellow, 4 purple
   1" x 6" rectangle – 2 yellow, 2 purple
   1" x 2" rectangle – 4 yellow, 2 purple
   2" x 2" square – 2 yellow
   2" x 4" rectangle – 1 yellow

Block 2 (top right):
   Template I – 8 turquoise, 4 purple, 8 tan, 2 gold

5" x 5" square – 4 tan
1" x 8" rectangle – 2 turquoise, 2 purple
Template W – 2 peach, 1 red, 1 blue

Block 3 (bottom left):
   Template I – 4 purple, 4 blue, 8 tan
   1" x 8" rectangle – 2 blue, 2 purple
   5" x 5" square – 4 tan
   1" x 2" rectangle – 2 green, 4 blue
   1" x 3" rectangle – 4 blue
   1" x 4" rectangle – 2 green
   1" x 1" square – 4 blue
   1" x 6" rectangle – 2 green
   2" x 8" rectangle – 1 green

Remember to add ¼" seam allowance to all templates, even the square and rectangle sizes. The sizes given for the triangles, rectangles, and squares are finished sizes.
When the directions read 4 Template T and Tr, it means cut 4 from Template T and then cut four more by flipping the Template over (Template Tr).

Block 4 (bottom right):

Template I – 4 purple, 4 tan

Template B – 4 red, 4 tan

Template J, Jr – 2 each peach, 2 each purple

4" x 5" rectangle – 4 tan

Border:

A drawing for the border of Project #14 does not appear at the back of the book. If you wish to try different colors, use the drawing included with the project instructions.

Template X – 5 medium beige

Template I – 4 background beige

Template O – 24 background beige

Template AA – 4 medium beige

Template BB – 4 background beige

Template Z – 24 medium beige

Template Y, Yr – 24 each background beige

Template CC – 24 dark brown

Template V, Vr – 24 each background beige

FABRIC REQUIREMENTS

One yard of tan is needed for the blocks. The other amounts are small pieces. For the border, 1 yard of dark brown is required. Two yards of the background beige are needed for the border. One-half yard of medium beige is ample for the border.

SEWING DIRECTIONS

Sew the blocks together first. These stars are very easy to construct. Study the piecing diagrams. I prefer to sew the centers of the stars first and then add the sides and top and bottom to the center unit.

For the border sew a V and Vr to either side of a CC (this makes Unit 1). Sew a Y, and Yr to either side of Z (this makes a Unit 2). Sew Unit 1 to Unit 2 to make one-half of the largest border section. You need 24 of these. Sew an O to each of the 4 corners of X. Repeat five times. Sew an O to AA. Sew BB to this. Sew an I onto that completed unit. This gives you one of the four corner units. Repeat three more times. Study the piecing diagram and sew your individual units together to form the complete border sections.

QUILTING

Parallel lines are the main type of quilting in this wall quilt. Meander quilting appears in the beige background fabric.

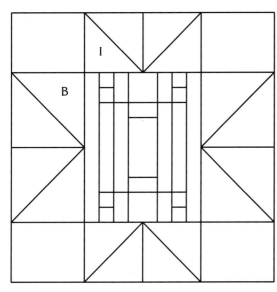

Block 1.

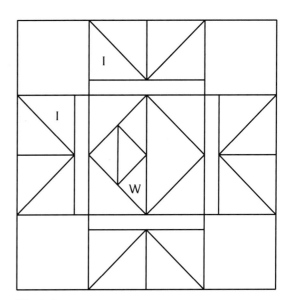

Block 2.

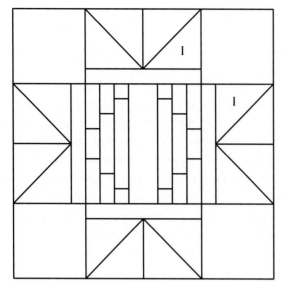

Block 3.

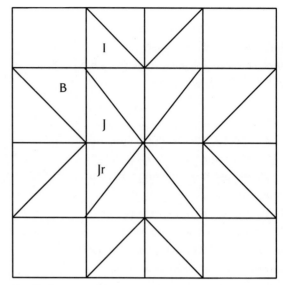

Block 4.

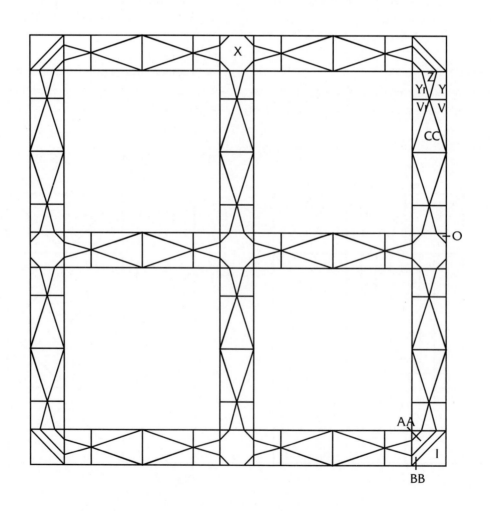

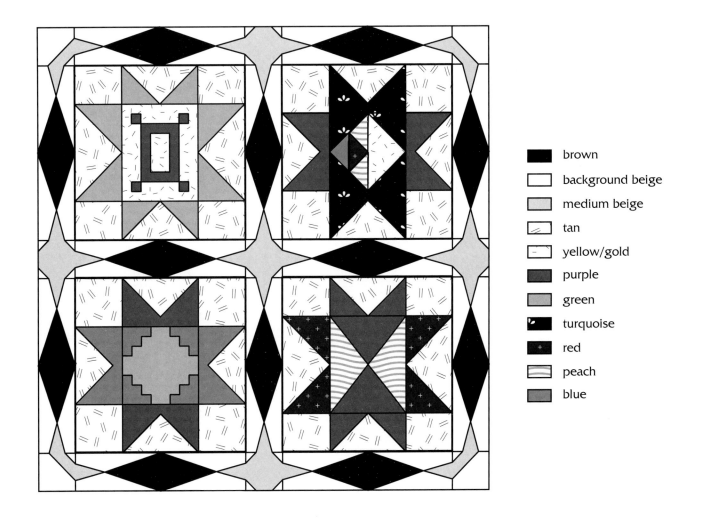

brown
background beige
medium beige
tan
yellow/gold
purple
green
turquoise
red
peach
blue

✦ LINE DRAWINGS OF BLOCKS AND BORDERS ✦

Project 1

Project 4

Project 2

Project 5

Project 3

Project 6

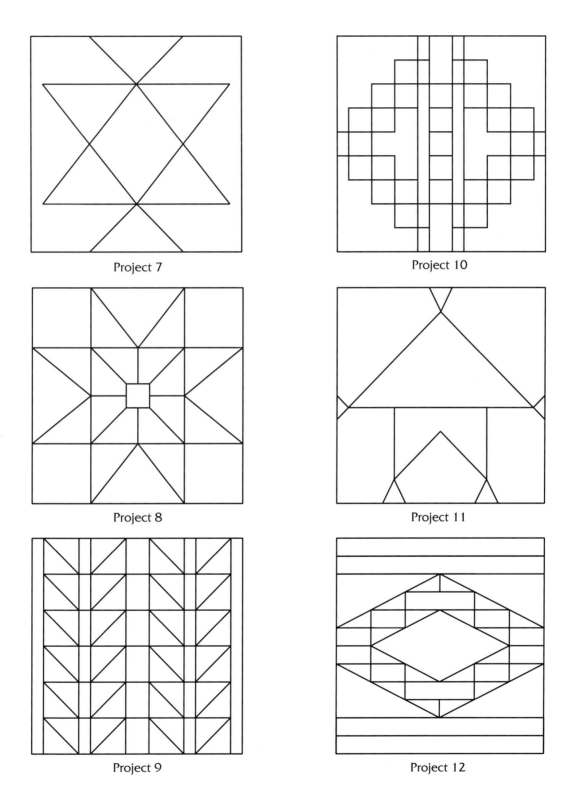

Project 7

Project 10

Project 8

Project 11

Project 9

Project 12

Project 13

Project 13

Project 13

Project 13

Project 14

Project 14

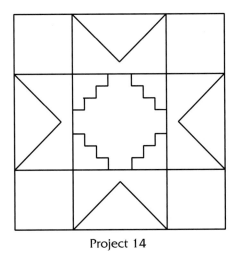

Project 14

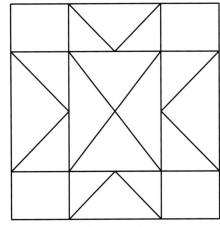

Project 14

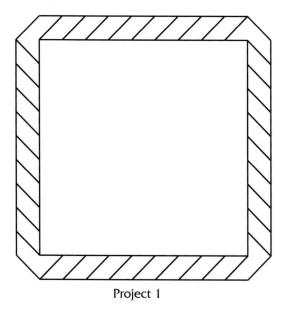

Project 1

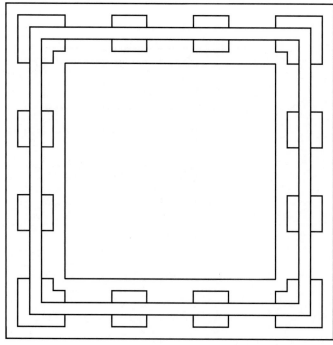

Project 3

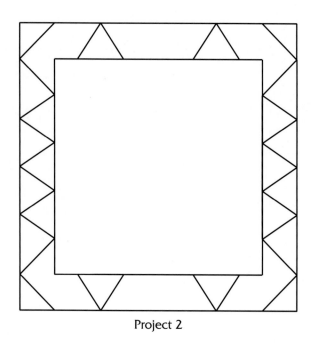

Project 2

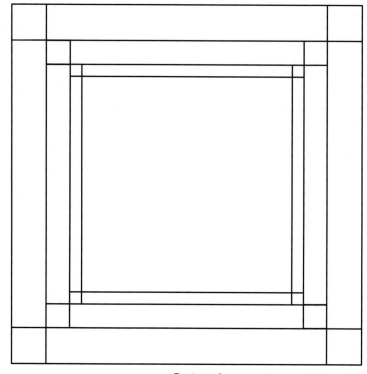

Project 4

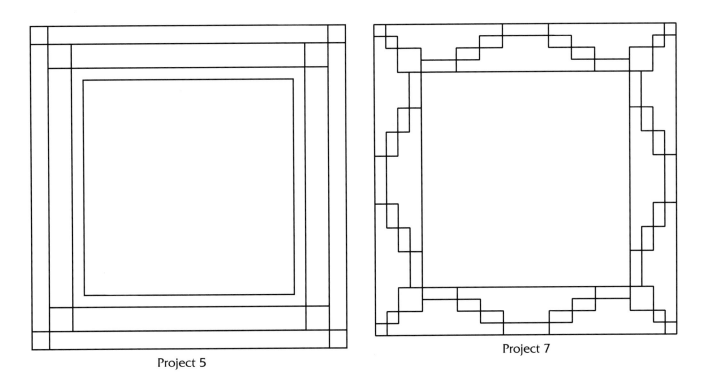

Project 5

Project 7

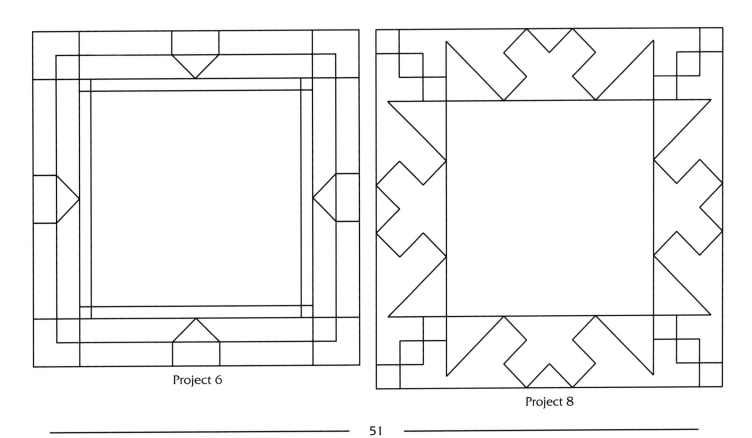

Project 6

Project 8

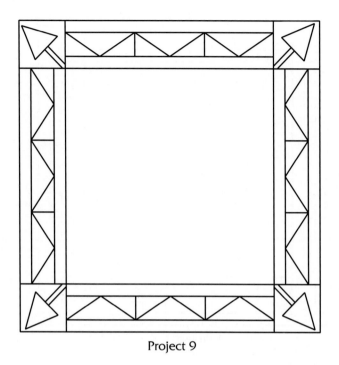

Project 9

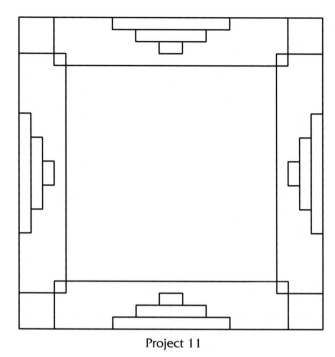

Project 11

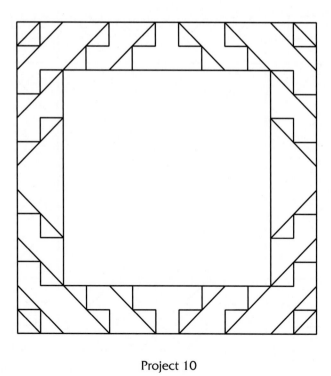

Project 10

Project 12

✧ ADDITIONAL BLOCKS WITH PIECING DIAGRAMS ✦

This section is for intermediate level quilters. It provides creative options for quilters. Many additional blocks are provided so that you may design original quilt projects. Try combining various blocks with different borders. Try placing different blocks next to one another. Make multiple copies of the same block and see how they look when placed together.

In order to provide the maximum number of designs to the readers, the scale for the drawings is based on 8-square-to-the-inch graph paper. If you find this size difficult to work with, you can take all these pages to a copy store and enlarge them 150%. This means you will work with a 4-square-to-the-inch grid.

To determine which templates you will need to construct any block or border, follow the basic directions given for the first block on the left side of this page. All blocks on the right side of the pages in this section show the construction/piecing lines. Such drawings show how a block is broken down into units of triangles, squares, and rectangles that are sewn together to form a block.

Directions:

•Photocopy the page with the black graph lines (located at the end of this section) The blocks and borders are all drawn to the scale of 1 square = 1 inch with 8 squares per inch.

•Lay this graph paper on your light table or light source.

•Make copies of any blocks you want to sew.

•Line up your block so the outside edges line up directly on top of the lines of the graph paper. The graph lines are shown in gray on this drawing on the following page.

•The three templates needed for this block are as follows (no seam allowances are added):

Template 1 – 2" x 3" rectangle
(Remember actual templates are not

Original Native American
Block Design

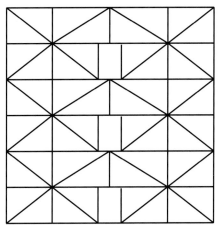

Piecing Diagram

provided for squares and rectangles that would normally be cut with a rotary cutter. Also these measurements do not include the seam allowances.)

Template C, Cr – 3" x 4" triangle

Template K, Kr – 3" x 5" triangle

The sizes were calculated by counting the squares on each side of the triangle or rectangle. One square equals 1 inch.

•These triangle templates are found in the template pages of the book.

•There is an exploded diagram that shows the basic method of construction for a block. Triangles are sewn together to form a square or rectangle. A design is broken down into rows or units. Rows can be added vertically as well as horizontally.

The blocks on page 55 illustrate the idea of shading in the blocks in different ways. The first shaded block shows the original Indian design as it was adapted from a cornhusk bag. The second line drawing shows the piecing diagram with all the extra lines for construction added. The last two blocks on the page show two more variations on how the design could be shaded by quilters. There are certainly other possibilities. Just make copies of the drawings and get out your colored pencils and have fun. Be sure to use the piecing diagram for the coloring. If you wish to get more creative, you can add or subtract lines to produce more variations.

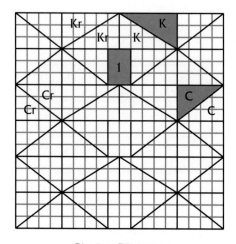

Piecing Diagram
Showing Templates
and Graph Paper Background

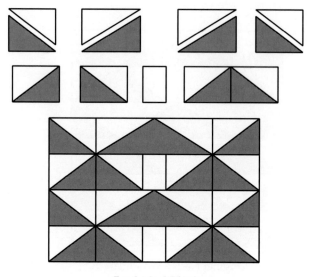

Exploded Block

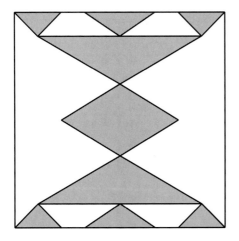

Original Native American Design

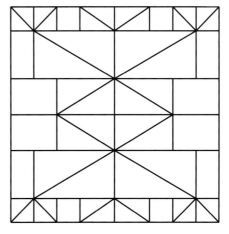

Piecing Diagram

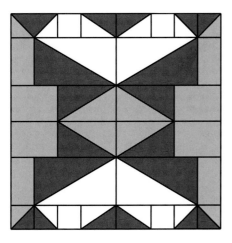

Variation #1

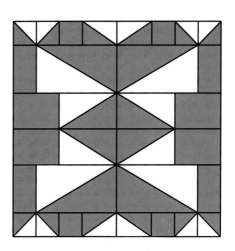

Variation #2

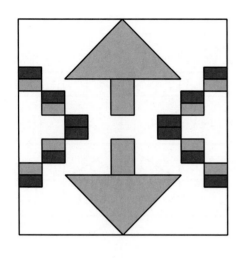

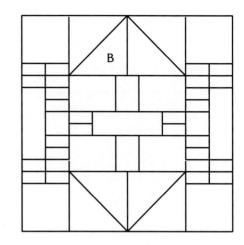

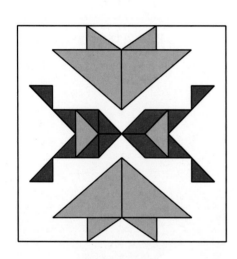

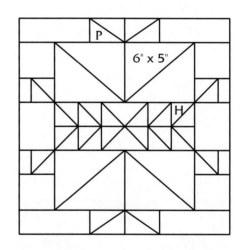

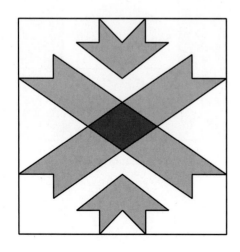

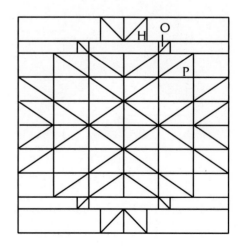

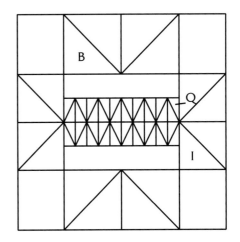

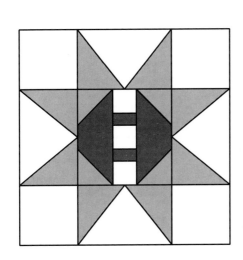

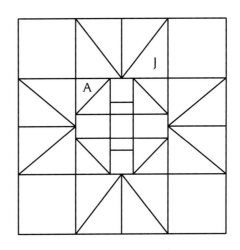

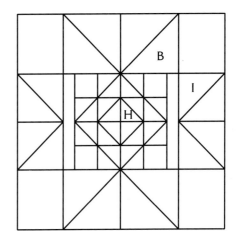

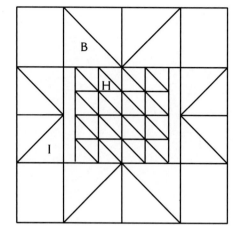

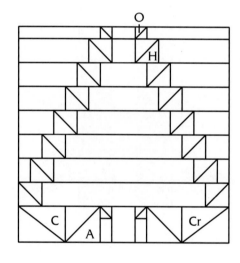

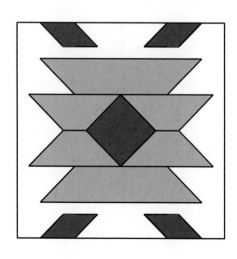

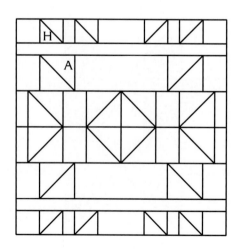

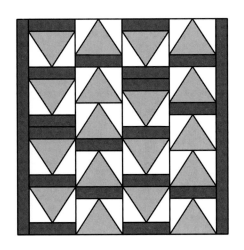

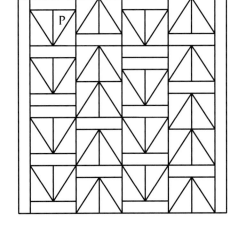

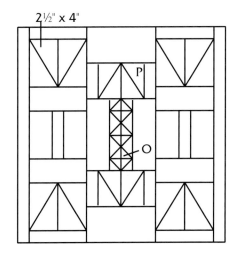

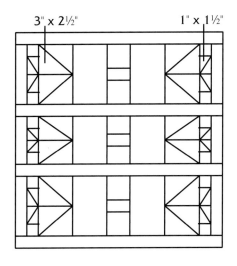

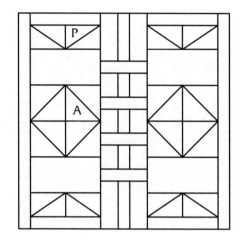

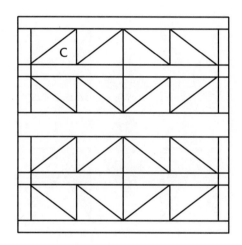

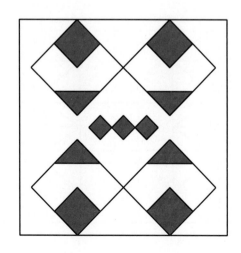

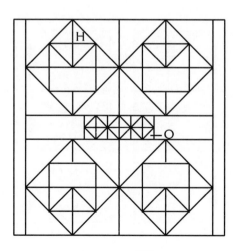

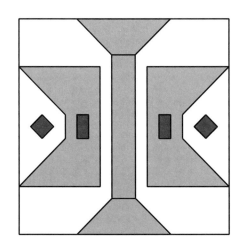

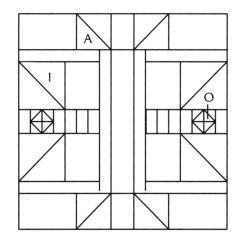

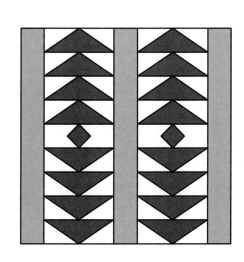

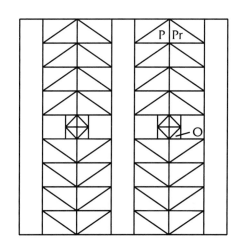

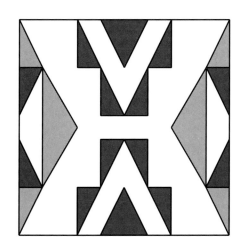

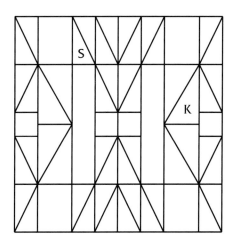

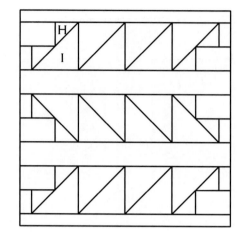

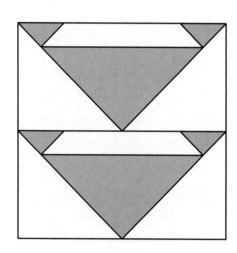

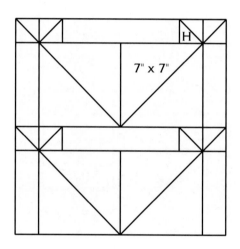

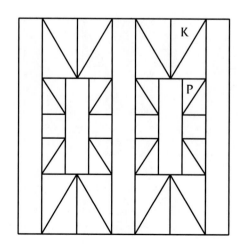

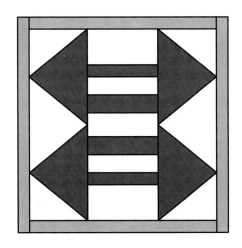

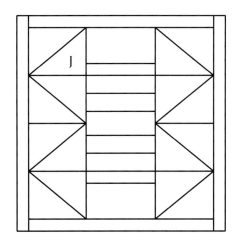

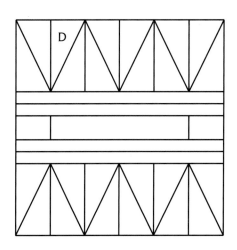

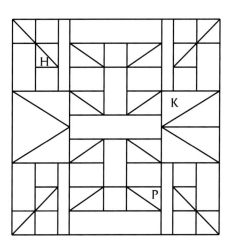

✢ TEMPLATES ✣

Templates are not provided for squares and rectangles that would normally be cut with a rotary cutter.

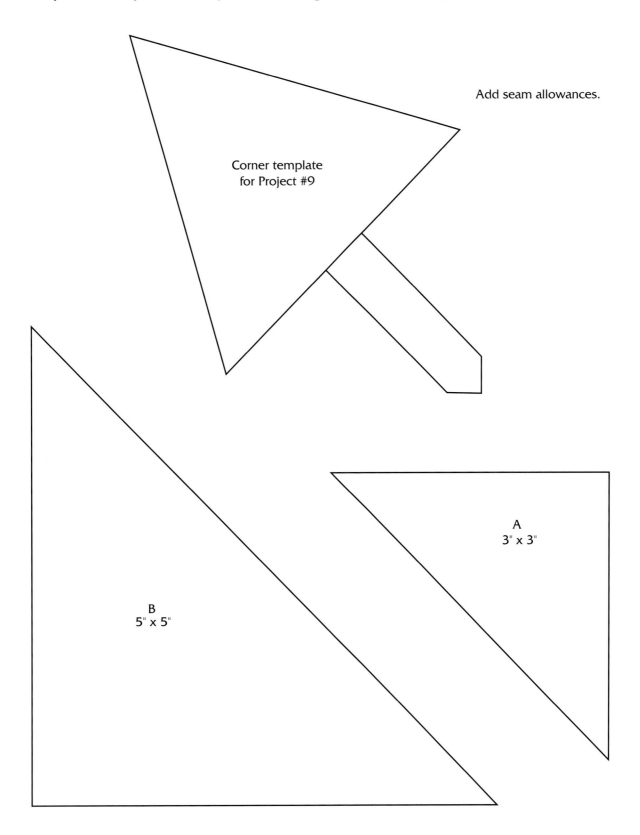

Add seam allowances.

Corner template
for Project #9

A
3" x 3"

B
5" x 5"

Add seam allowances.

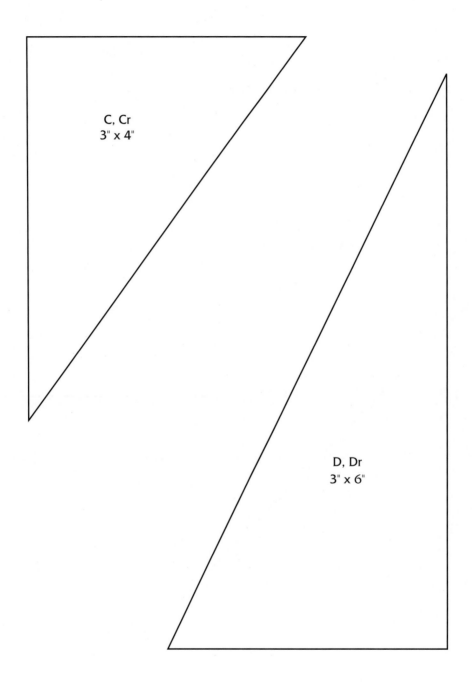

C, Cr
3" x 4"

D, Dr
3" x 6"

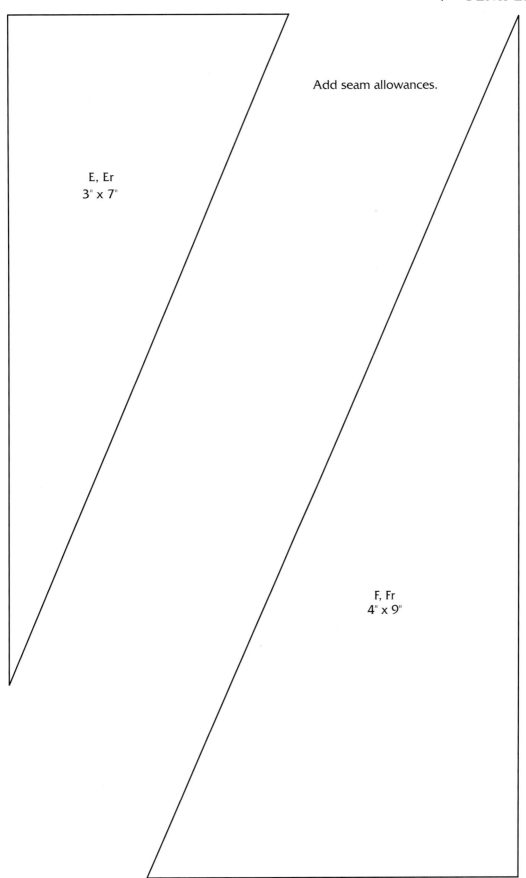

Add seam allowances.

E, Er
3" x 7"

F, Fr
4" x 9"

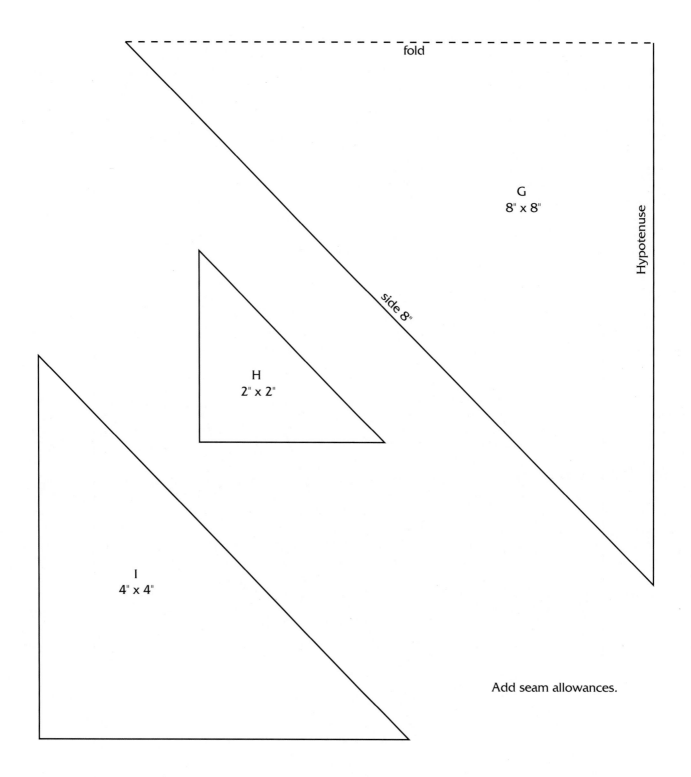

fold

G
8" x 8"

Hypotenuse

side 8"

H
2" x 2"

I
4" x 4"

Add seam allowances.

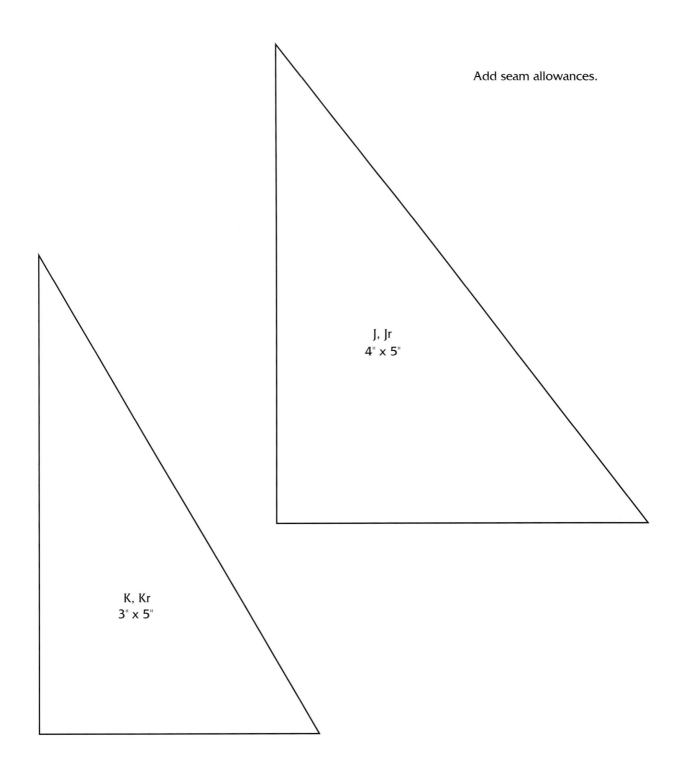

Add seam allowances.

J, Jr
4" x 5"

K, Kr
3" x 5"

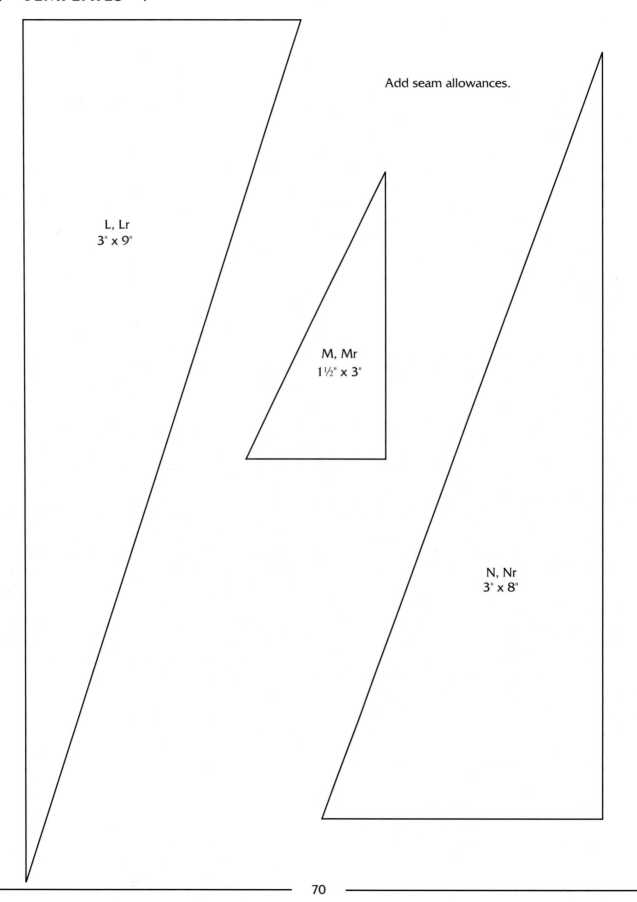

Add seam allowances.

L, Lr
3" x 9"

M, Mr
1½" x 3"

N, Nr
3" x 8"

Add seam allowances.

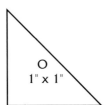

O
1" x 1"

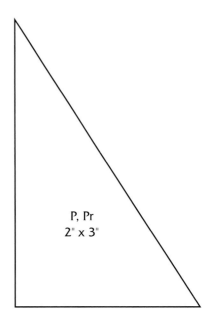

P, Pr
2" x 3"

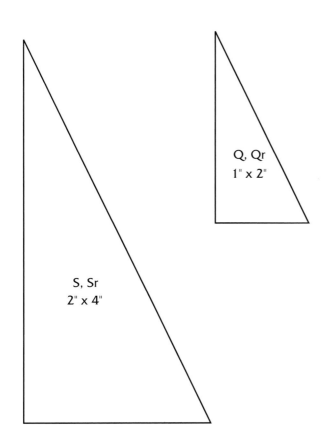

Q, Qr
1" x 2"

S, Sr
2" x 4"

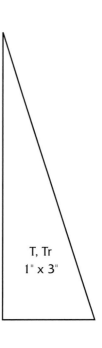

T, Tr
1" x 3"

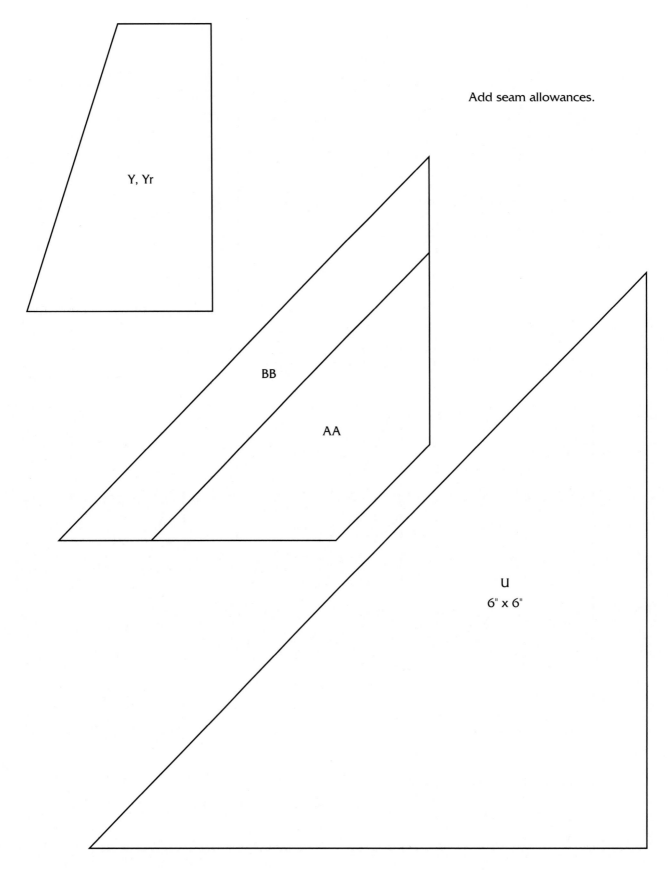

Add seam allowances.

Y, Yr

BB

AA

U
6" x 6"

Add seam allowances.

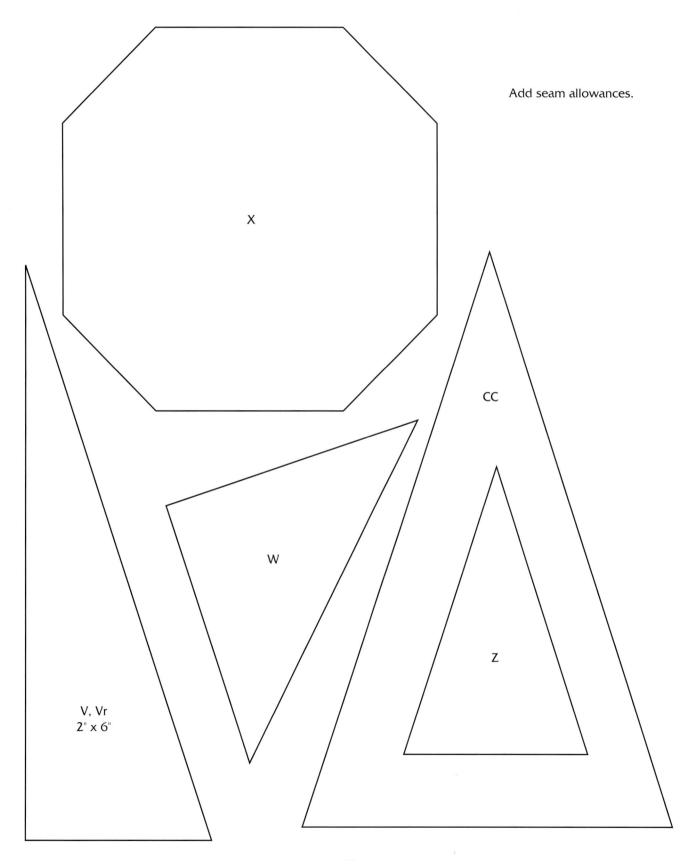

X

CC

W

Z

V, Vr
2" x 6"

✦ QUILTING MOTIFS ✦

Reprinted from *Quilt Almanac* 1992.

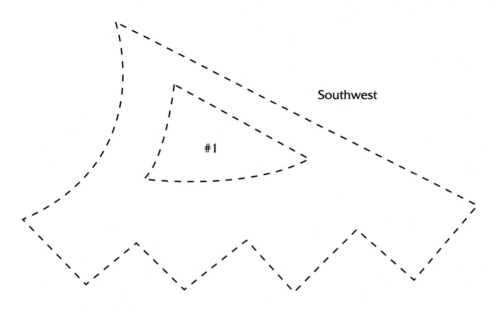

Southwest

#1

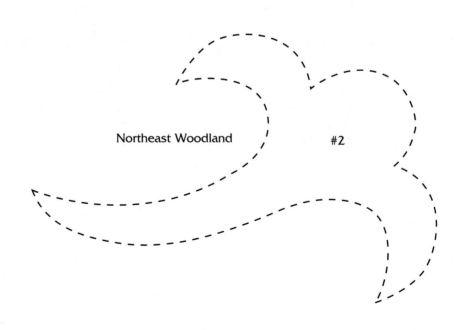

Northeast Woodland

#2

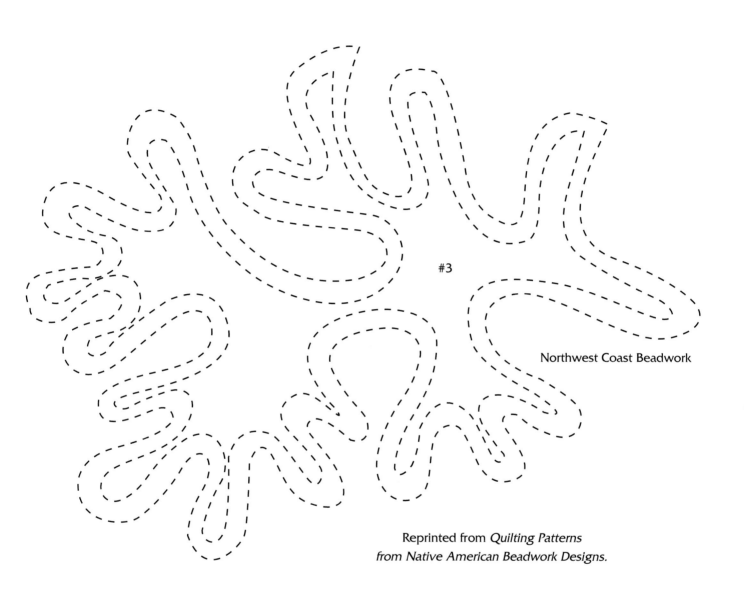

#3

Northwest Coast Beadwork

Reprinted from *Quilting Patterns
from Native American Beadwork Designs.*

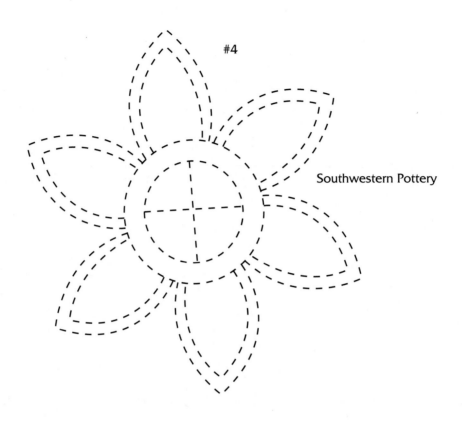

#4

Southwestern Pottery

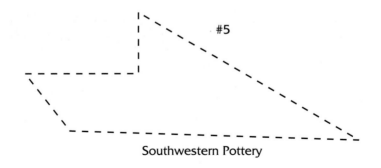

#5

Southwestern Pottery

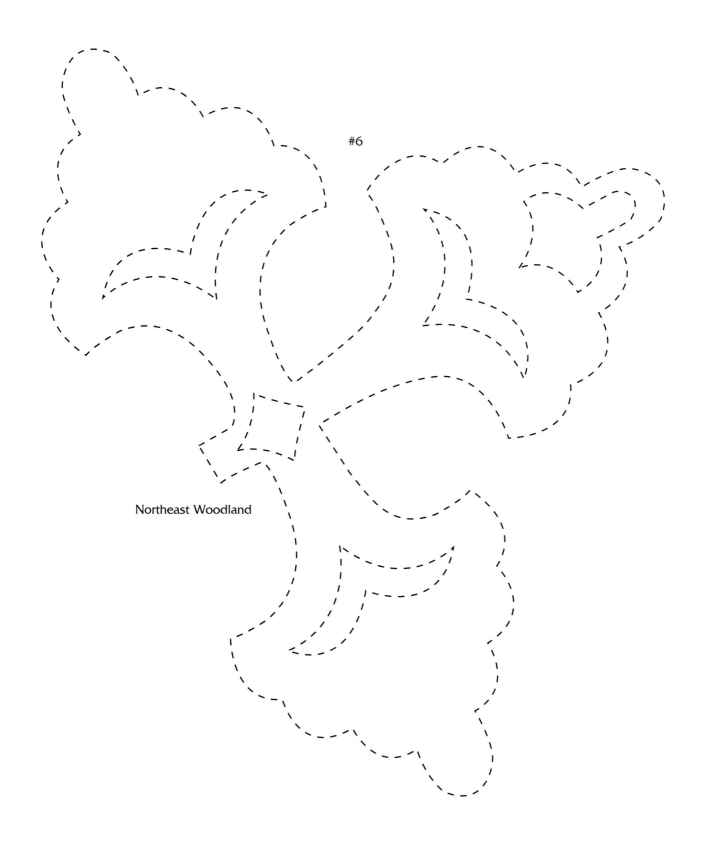

#6

Northeast Woodland

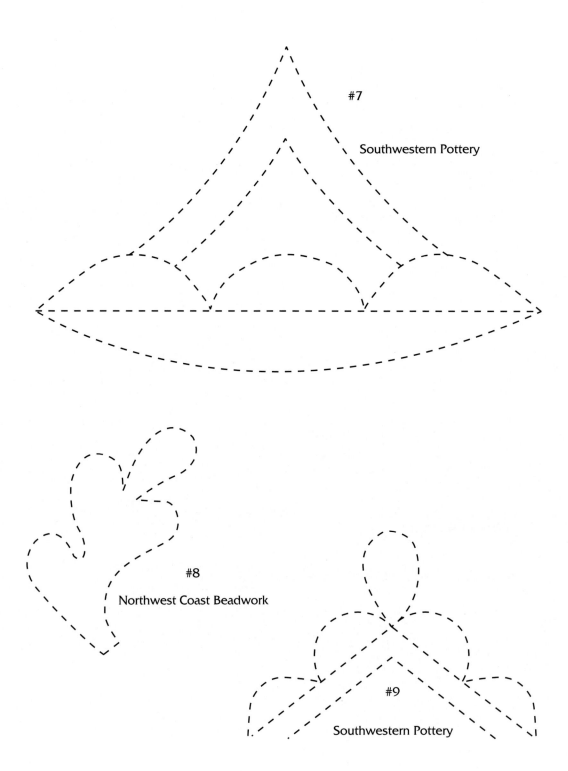

#7

Southwestern Pottery

#8

Northwest Coast Beadwork

#9

Southwestern Pottery

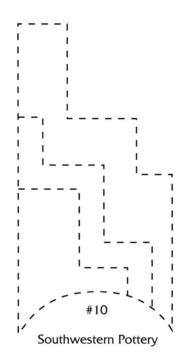

#10

Southwestern Pottery

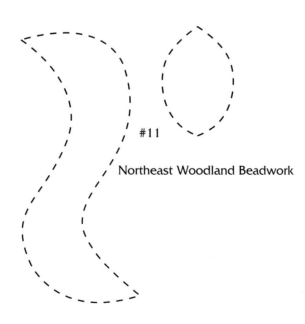

#11

Northeast Woodland Beadwork

∽ American Quilter's Society ∾

dedicated to publishing books for today's quilters

*These books can be found in local bookstores and quilt shops. If you are unable to locate a title
in your area, you can order by mail from AQS, P.O. Box 3290, Paducah, KY 42002-3290.
Please add $1 for the first book and 40¢ for each additional one to cover postage and handling.
(International orders please add $1.50 for the first book and $1 for each additional one.)*